CHEAT CODE

CHEAT CODE

How to Win with Money
Before Adulting Hits Hard

LINDSEY BAKER, MAT
JOE BAKER, MBA

Paperback ISBN (KDP): 979-8-9930533-1-8
Paperback ISBN (Ingram): 979-8-9930533-7-0
eBook ISBN: 979-8-9930533-0-1

YAN040000   YOUNG ADULT NONFICTION / Personal Finance
BUS050030   BUSINESS & ECONOMICS / Personal Finance / Money Management
EDU029040   EDUCATION / Teaching / Subjects / Social Science

Cover design and typesetting by Kaitlin Barwick

themoneycheatcode.com

To all our former students —

You inspired this journey.

May you always chase your dreams
and take charge of your future.

Contents

CONTENTS

CONTENTS

A Word from the Authors

Joe Baker

I grew up on a little farm just outside of Emerson, Arkansas. If you've never heard of it, don't feel bad—there were only about 393 people living there at the time! Life on our farm included me, my family, a bunch of dogs, some chickens, a few cows, and a couple of horses. And just for the record, yes, we had an outhouse instead of a real bathroom until I was 9 years old. Fun fact: It had *two* holes. Fancy, right?

Even though life was simple and we didn't have much money, it never really crossed my mind that we were "poor." It was just normal life. I do remember once asking my granny about the fancy country club we drove by. She laughed and said, "Honey, you have to have a bathtub full of money to go there." That stuck with me for a long time.

College wasn't really a thing in my family, and no one expected me to go. But I didn't want to work construction with my dad or haul hay for six cents a bale forever. Yes, six cents. And no, my dad didn't pay me for working for him. He said, "You're getting paid every time you eat at my table!" Classic dad move.

Luckily, there was a small college just 15 miles away. I became a first-generation college graduate by juggling two or three jobs at a time while staying actively involved on campus. I wasn't at the top of my college class, but I was elected Student Body President my senior year!

Fast forward and I earned my MBA, spent over 20 years teaching personal finance as an adjunct instructor, retired from a successful career in insurance and financial services, and traveled the country as a speaker, promoting financial literacy to both academic and corporate audiences.

This is what I tell my students: You do not have to come from money to build a great life. You do not have to be the smartest person in the room. You do not have to get everything perfect the first time. But if you learn a few key lessons about money early, and stick with them, you'll be amazed where you can go.

That's what this book is all about—making sure you have the tools to build a future you're proud of. Let's get started!

Lindsey Baker

Back in college, I didn't have a car, bills, or much responsibility to my name. I had a little savings from working at a daycare and picking up odd jobs during high school, but all my basic needs were covered while I was at school. The real world still felt pretty far away.

One of my required college classes was Personal Finance. I remember sitting there, half-listening to a professor drone on about financial terms, completely unable to connect with anything he was saying. His lectures were dry, full of technical jargon, and felt miles away from anything happening in my life. Somehow, I squeaked out a B in that class.

It wasn't until after college that I realized how important that class actually was, not just for what it taught me but for everything it didn't. Looking back, I had never taken a single class in high school that taught me how money really works. Not budgeting. Not credit. Not investing. Nothing. And that gap followed me into adulthood.

That's when I started to see the bigger issue. In many schools across the country, young people aren't being taught about money in a way that actually prepares them for life.

It hit even harder when I finally started listening to my dad. I had heard his advice for years, but I never truly listened. Not until I had to. And once I did, everything started to click.

With over a decade of experience teaching middle and high school students, I've learned how to make tough concepts feel relatable and practical. That's exactly what I set out to do with this book. Just remember, your report card doesn't determine how well you'll handle money in the real world. Financial success isn't about your grades; it's about your habits.

Financial literacy is a lifelong class. And you have the chance to pass it with flying colors.

LEVEL UP!

Your Financial Power Starts Here

Let's get one thing straight: We teach *a lot* of stuff in school. Some of it's important. Some of it's . . . **throws hands up**
You've probably had to:

- Memorize the parts of a volcano
- Study ancient civilizations
- Convert Fahrenheit to Celsius

But you know what most schools *haven't* taught?

→ How credit cards really work
  (spoiler: they're not free money)
→ How to apply for jobs
→ How to make your money *make more money*
→ How to become financially independent so you can live life on *your* terms

We teach about the Silk Road, but not how to budget.
We teach Shakespeare, but not how to open a bank account.
We teach the square root of 144, but not how to pay rent.
Like . . . hello?
Financial literacy in the US has hovered around 50% for the past eight years, showing little to no improvement.[1]

---

1. Michelle Meineke, "Can You Answer These 3 Questions About Your Finances? The Majority of US Adults Cannot," World Economic Forum, April 24, 2024, https://www.weforum.org/stories/2024/04/financial-literacy-money-education/.

That means half of American adults don't understand the basics of money. This isn't just some boring stat; it's a red flag. If we don't know how to manage money, we can't build strong futures, buy homes, avoid debt, or retire comfortably.

For young people like you, this matters *right now*. Because if your generation doesn't learn how money works, we'll keep repeating the same mistakes. And the cost isn't just personal. A financially uneducated population weakens our economy, widens the wealth gap, and limits what our country can achieve. You can't afford to sit this one out. Learning about money is one of the most powerful things you can do for yourself and for the future of society.

But . . . personal finance is *finally* starting to get the spotlight it deserves. States across the US are waking up and realizing, "Hey, maybe we should teach students how money works before they're 25 and buried in credit card debt." Shocking idea, right?

Some states have made personal finance *required* to graduate. *claps for them* Others are catching up. But no matter where you live, here's the truth:

Money affects *every single part* of your future.

Want to travel the world?

Start a business?

Buy cool stuff without worrying about bills?

Help your family out?

Not live paycheck to paycheck for the rest of your life?

You're going to need money skills to do that.

This book is your launchpad. We're not here to throw boring vocabulary at you. (However, all bolded terms are defined in the glossary at the end of the book.) Instead, we're here to show you how to:

→ **Make money**
→ **Keep money**
→ **Grow money**

And most importantly, we'll teach you how to use it to build the life you want. Not your parents' life. Not your teacher's. Yours.

Whether you want to become a millionaire or just not stress about bills all the time, this stuff matters. You don't need to be a math genius or a Wall Street bro. You just need to care a *little* bit now . . . so your future self can say, "Wow. I'm glad I learned that when I did."

Why should you care about money, *even if you don't yet?*

Because the world runs on it. And you're going to be in the world for a long time.

So let's get to it. Let's unlock your financial power.

Let's level up.

Curtis "Wall Street" Carroll: From Illiteracy to Financial Freedom

In 1996, at just 17 years old, Curtis was sentenced to 54 years to life for killing a man during an armed robbery. Growing up in Oakland, California, he never really had a chance. Raised by drug dealers and surviving on the streets, he was taught one core belief early on: "If you have money, you have power."

But back then, Curtis didn't know how to actually get money and definitely not the right way.

That would all start to change in the most unlikely place: San Quentin State Prison.

Sitting alone in his prison cell, Curtis Carroll made a decision: He would teach himself how to read. It was painful, slow, and frustrating, but through pure willpower, he figured it out.

Once he unlocked the ability to read, he set his sights even higher. Curtis started devouring the financial sections of newspapers, learning the language of investing, stocks, and the money game.

Other inmates began to notice, and he earned the nickname, "Wall Street."

But Curtis didn't stop there. He made it his mission to fight against financial illiteracy, not just for himself but for everyone around him.

In his TED Talk, Curtis says it plain and clear:

"Financial illiteracy is a disease that has crippled minorities and the lower class in our society for generations, and we should be furious about that."

He asks a powerful question:

"How can 50% of Americans be financially illiterate in a nation built on financial prosperity?"

The truth is, not knowing how money works is a national crisis. It holds people back. It limits dreams. And it hurts the future of our whole society.

Curtis Carroll believes that when people understand money, they unlock freedom. Not just financial freedom but freedom to make better choices, chase bigger dreams, and change their futures.[2]

He believes that the steps to financial freedom aren't easy, but they aren't a mystery either.

Anyone can learn them.

Anyone can change their story.

Widespread financial literacy can transform lives, especially for those who have been forgotten, underestimated, or written off by society.

---

2. Curtis Carroll "Wall Street," "How I Learned to Read—and Trade Stocks—in Prison," TED, January 2016, https://www.ted.com/talks/curtis_wall_street_carroll_how_i_learned_to_read_and_trade_stocks_in_prison.

And it all starts with a decision: To learn. To grow. To take
control of your future.

1

Build a Life You Don't Want to Escape From

You've probably been asked this question before:

"What do you want to do after high school?"

And if that question makes you want to hide under a hoodie and disappear, you're not alone.

Maybe your answer is something like:

- "Get a job so I can move out."
- "Go to college . . . I think?"
- "Make money."
- "No clue. Can I just sleep for a year first?"

No shame in any of those answers.

But here's the thing: A job title or paycheck might sound nice, but it's not everything. We live in a world that tells you to climb the ladder, but nobody teaches you how to make sure the ladder is even leaning against the right wall.

It's time to stop chasing someone else's version of success and start building a path that actually means something to *you*.

Before you can chase your dream life, you need your basics covered: food, shelter, safety, community, and mental health.

Once those are in place, you can reach for more[1]:

→ Self-actualization = Becoming everything you're capable of becoming.
→ Transcendence = Doing something that's bigger than just you.

So, yes, money matters. But not because it makes you "successful." It matters because it helps you build the kind of life where you *can* grow, create, help, explore, thrive, and transcend.

Your Job Is Not Your Identity

Long ago, surnames were often tied to a person's role in society. Names like *Baker*, *Smith*, or *Taylor* were clear indicators of someone's occupation. If your last name was *Baker*, chances are your family made bread for generations. These labels helped define a person's place in the community.[2]

Today, one of the first things people ask is, "So, what do you do?"

Translation: *How do you earn your worth in the world? What's your label, your status, your role in the system?*

But at the core of it all, you are not your job. You are not your surname.

You can be a teacher who writes novels. A welder who starts a podcast. An IT specialist who surfs on weekends and volunteers at animal shelters. You're allowed to be and do more than one thing.

Work can be a stepping stone, a calling, just a way to make money—or all three. The goal is to figure out how to make it work for *you*.

---

1. Saul McLeod, PhD, "Maslow's Hierarchy of Needs," *Simply Psychology*, March 14, 2025, https://www.simply psychology.org/maslow.
2. "Why Do We Have Surnames?" *English Heritage*, July 8, 2016, https://www.english-heritage.org.uk/.

The World of Work Has Changed

Thirty years ago, no one was making a living creating Minecraft videos or selling handmade sneakers online. Today? Entire careers exist that didn't back then. Welcome to the creator economy.

New roles pop up all the time like content creators, app designers, streamers, crypto consultants, and community managers.[3]

Some work in offices. Others work from coffee shops, bedrooms, or beaches.

Technology has kicked open a lot of doors. Now the challenge is walking through the right one for you.

Before chasing a job you think you "should" want, ask yourself:

- ☐ What makes you feel excited?
- ☐ What do you get lost in doing?
- ☐ What are you curious about, even when no one's making you do it?
- ☐ If you monetize that passion, could it burn out?

You're going to spend a lot of time in whatever career path you choose, so it's ideal if you enjoy what you do. But what many people don't predict is that passion doesn't always last forever. Life changes, and so can your interests. You might find yourself wanting to switch directions completely someday, and that's totally okay. It's also perfectly valid to take a job just to pay the bills, even if it's not your dream job.

Surviving and staying stable is just as important as chasing your passion.

Job vs. Career vs. Calling vs. Gig

There's no one right way to earn a living. Check out the different paths people take:

---

3. See Creator Economy Jobs for active job listings in creative roles: https://www.creatoreconomyjobs.co/

Type	What It Is	When It Makes Sense
Job	Pays the bills	You need money now
Gig	Short-term, flexible	You want freedom or side income
Career	Long-term growth	You want structure and goals
Calling	Deep purpose	You want your work to reflect your values

Guess what? You don't have to choose just one. Most people bounce between these at different times. Your path can evolve, change direction, or combine all four.

Money Isn't the Goal—It's the Tool

Bottom line: You don't need to obsess over every penny.

But you *do* need to understand that every dollar you spend shapes your future.

Here's a truth bomb:

Money = Freedom

BUT

Freedom = Trade-offs

Want to travel the world? Cool. Maybe pass on the $6-a-day iced latte for a while.

Want to start your own business? Awesome. That might mean living a little leaner at first.

These aren't sacrifices. These are *power moves*.

When you know what you want, you get to spend with *intention*. That's when money stops controlling you and starts working *for* you.

10 Financial Mistakes Young Adults Make

1. Not having financial goals
2. Thinking more money will solve all their problems
3. Not building credit responsibly
4. Not investing sooner
5. Overpaying for college or not understanding loans
6. Letting comparison steal their financial strategy
7. Falling for get-rich-quick schemes
8. Not asking questions
9. Not thinking long term
10. Ignoring financial education because it feels inaccessible

We've got you. The rest of this book will help you avoid those common money mistakes and unlock the cheat code to smart money moves.

LEVEL UP

YOUR LIFE, YOUR BLUEPRINT

Grab a journal or notebook to use throughout this journey.

On the first page, answer this: If money weren't a problem, what would you do every day?

List three things you'd love to do, places you'd want to live, or big goals you'd chase. Don't hold back.

Now pick one of those goals. Ask yourself: What's one small step I could take this week to get just a little closer to it—say, 1%?

Keep it simple. One action. One move forward.

This week, I will: _____

Sara Blakely: Fail Big, Win Bigger

Before she was a billionaire, before Oprah gave her product the green light, and before the name SPANX was in anyone's vocabulary, Sara Blakely was just trying to figure life out.

She thought she'd go to law school. She studied hard, signed up for the LSAT . . . and failed. Not once, but twice. That might've demoralized most people, but it just sent Sara in a different direction.

Instead of forcing a path that wasn't working, she pivoted. She moved into a commission-only job selling fax machines door to door in Florida's scorching heat. Imagine business shoes, rejection after rejection, and no air conditioning. Sara learned fast how to take a "no" and keep going. That job gave her something priceless: thick skin and grit.[4]

And that would come in handy.

One day, Sara wanted to wear her white pants but couldn't find any undergarment that didn't bunch, roll, or show through. So she grabbed a pair of pantyhose, cut the feet off, and wore them under her pants. The idea stuck: what if this quick fix could be a real product?

She didn't tell anyone her idea for a year. Not her friends and not her coworkers because she didn't want to risk hearing, "That'll never work," before she had even tried. With no business degree, no product design background, and just $5,000 in savings, she quietly began building what would become a billion-dollar brand.[5]

She cold-called factories. Most said no. One *finally* gave her a shot.

4. Gillian Zoe Segal, "This Self-Made Billionaire Failed the LSAT Twice, Then Sold Fax Machines for 7 Years before Hitting Big-Here's How She Got There," CNBC, April 3, 2019, https://www.cnbc.com/2019/04/03/self-made -billionaire-spanx-founder-sara-blakely-sold-fax-machines-before-making-it-big.html.
5. Sydney Lake, "Spanx Founder Sara Blakely's $1 Billion Idea Started with Just $5,000 in Savings and Wanting to Solve Her Own Problem," *Fortune*, February 27, 2024, https://fortune.com/2024/02/27/sara-blakely-spanx -billion-dollar-idea-oprah-5000-savings-billionaire/.

But the foundation of her grit was built long before any of that—at her family's dinner table.

Her dad had a tradition. Every week, he'd ask: "What did you fail at this week?"

And if Sara and her brother had nothing to report, he'd actually be disappointed.

He didn't want his kids to fear failure. He wanted them to try, to stretch, to experiment. He helped them understand that real failure wasn't about messing up; rather it was about not trying in the first place.[6]

That mindset became a core part of how Sara operated. She saw failure as a launchpad, not a wall. SPANX only exists because she bombed the LSAT and kept going through rejections, awkward pitches, and industry pushback. She never let fear make her small.

Today, Sara Blakely is one of the most successful self-made entrepreneurs in the world. She built her company from the ground up with no loans, no outside investors, no permission needed.

She didn't wait for someone to approve her idea.

She didn't need the perfect resume or the perfect timing.

She just started. And she kept going.

6. Taylor Locke, "Why Spanx Founder Sara Blakely Hid Her Billion-Dollar Business Idea from Friends and Family for a Year," CNBC, August 10, 2020, https://www.cnbc.com/2020/02/06/why-spanxs-sara-blakely-kept-billion-dollar-idea-secret.

A WORD FROM
LINDSEY BAKER

Growing up, I always hated the question: "What do you want to be?"

It felt like everyone else had a five-step plan to their future, while I was just winging it one day at a time.

Even in college, I never had a clear "calling." I knew I loved reading, writing, and anything in the humanities. I knew I wanted to travel and see the world. What I didn't want? To become a teacher, because that's what my mom did, and I was determined to do something different.

I graduated following a recession, and the job market was slow. But I had curiosity and Wi-Fi. So I started digging online and found a path I hadn't considered: teaching English abroad.

I had no clue what I was doing, but I signed up for a TEFL course and got certified. Then an online search led me to an old-school website called Dave's ESL Café. I scrolled through the international job board and spotted a teaching position in the Middle East and applied. After the acceptance, I waited to tell friends and family two weeks before I left. I didn't want anyone talking me out of it, and I needed to figure it out for myself.

That one decision changed everything. I ended up teaching in two different countries the next couple of years. I made a modest income. I was able to do a lot of backpacking. And—plot twist—I realized that I actually *loved* teaching.

Turns out, the job I thought I didn't want was exactly where I was supposed to be. And it laid the foundation for the rest of my career.

Trying something new helped me figure out what I was good at and what I wasn't. It taught me independence, resilience, and the value of new perspectives. The experience didn't just shape my career, it shaped me.

2

Appreciate
What Appreciates

Truth: You don't need to be rich to build wealth, but you *can* go broke trying to look rich.

Take NFL quarterback Kirk Cousins. Despite signing multi-million-dollar contracts with both the Minnesota Vikings and the Atlanta Falcons, he continued living in his in-laws' basement in Atlanta, drove a dented van inherited from his grandma for years, and later picked up a used Mercedes at a bargain.[7] Why? Because Kirk knows something most people don't:

It's not about what you earn.

It's about what you *keep* and *grow*.

Even with millions, people go broke when they spend on stuff that loses value.

Take this for example:

- NBA median salary: $6.7 million[8]
- NFL median salary: $860,000[9]

And yet . . .

7. Nidhi, "$180 Million QB Kirk Cousins Reveals He is Still Living in His In-Law's Basement in Atlanta," *The Sports Rush*, April 7, 2024, https://thesportsrush.com/nfl-news-180-million-qb-kirk-cousins-reveals-he-is-still-living-in-his-in-laws-basement-in-atlanta.
8. Ryan Phillips, "What's the Average NBA Salary for 2024–25 Season?" *SI*, September 18, 2024, https://www.si.com/nba/whats-average-nba-salary-for-2024-25-season.
9. Kerri Anne Renzulli, "Here's What the Average NFL Player Makes in a Season," CNBC, September 5, 2019, https://www.cnbc.com/2019/02/01/heres-what-the-average-nfl-players-makes-in-a-season.html.

- 60% of NBA players go broke within 5 years of retirement
- 78% of NFL players hit financial stress within just 2 years[10]

Why? Because many invest in lifestyle, not in assets.

Appreciable vs. Depreciable— Know the Difference

Let's break it down.

This chart shows what helps your money grow (**appreciate**) versus what drains it (**depreciate**).

Item	Type	Why It Matters
Financial investments (like index funds or ETFs)	**Appreciable**	Grows your money over time with compound interest
New car you finance at 12% interest	Depreciable	Loses value fast and adds debt
College degree (if chosen wisely)	**Appreciable**	Can raise lifetime earnings significantly
Designer sneakers you barely wear	Depreciable	Cool now, worthless later
Starting a small online business	**Appreciable**	Can turn into a steady source of income
Newest phone every year	Depreciable	Fun, but outdated fast and costs a lot
Real estate you rent out	**Appreciable**	Can build value and generate monthly income
$600 gaming console with no resale value	Depreciable	Entertainment only, no financial return

---

10. Chris Dudley, "Money Lessons Learned from Pro Athletes' Financial Fouls," CNBC, May 15, 2018, https://www.cnbc.com/2018/05/14/money-lessons-learned-from-pro-athletes-financial-fouls.html.

Item	Type	Why It Matters
Taking a course to learn a skill (coding, design, video editing)	**Appreciable**	Boosts your future earning potential
Fancy furniture for your bedroom	Depreciable	Looks nice, but loses value immediately and doesn't pay you back
Buying a camera to start a YouTube or photo biz	**Appreciable**	Turns into a tool to create content and potentially earn income

What This Means for *You*

You don't have to be in the NFL to fall into the same lifestyle trap.

The $70 hoodie you wore twice.

The $5 coffee every morning.

The gaming setup that cost more than your laptop for school.

It adds up.

So does *smart investing*, even if you're just starting small.

Real Moves to Make

- ☐ Choose investments over impulsive purchases
- ☐ Save for a laptop that helps you learn or earn, not one just for clout
- ☐ Pay off credit card debt instead of upgrading your phone
- ☐ Think "What value does this bring later?" not just, "Do I want it now?"

You don't have to live on ramen noodles or skip every fun thing. Just be intentional. Every dollar is a vote: Are you voting for comfort today or freedom tomorrow?

Lifestyle Creep: When your spending slowly increases as you start making more money, even if your needs haven't changed.

It's when things that used to feel like *treats* (new shoes, morning coffee, takeout on the weekend) start to feel normal or more regular, and suddenly, you're spending way more without realizing it.

Examples

You get a raise or start a part-time job, and instead of saving more, you start:

- Ordering Uber Eats every day
- Buying designer name brands instead
- Upgrading to premium economy
- Getting nails done every two weeks rather than four
- Adding new subscription plans
- Making more "I deserve it" purchases

. . . and now you're back to feeling broke again.

Lifestyle creep isn't a monster under your bed; it's the quiet way your spending grows . . . without you even realizing it.

Here's the thing:

I'm not here to tell you what you can or can't buy. That's not the move. What I do want you to see is this: Lifestyle creep shows up in the "I need this" moments that aren't really needs.

It's in the pressure to keep up with people who aren't even in your lane.

It's sneaky. And it adds up.

You see the new shoes, the concert tickets, the brand-new car, or that "just because" shopping haul on social media, and suddenly, your perfectly fine life starts to feel . . . not enough.

First, it was keeping up with the Joneses. Then it was keeping up with the Kardashians. Now? It's trying to keep up with some random influencer on TikTok who rented a Lamborghini for the day.

Before you know it, your money isn't following your goals. It's following someone else's highlight reel.

But when you start spending with intention, not emotion, you take back control. And that's when things really start to change.

LEVEL UP

Grab your notebook or journal again. This one's about real value—not just vibes.

Look at your last purchases. Pick 3 that felt like "must-haves" in the moment. Now be real: did they actually add long-term value?

Ask yourself: *Would I still buy this if I were working toward something big, like my own business, travel goals, or my first apartment?*

Now write down 3 things you could spend money on that would actually *appreciate* over time. These are things that could help you grow, earn, or learn.

What's one small action you can take this week to start spending more intentionally?

This week, I will: _____

Mike Tyson: From Knockouts to Knocked Out

At just 20 years old, Mike Tyson became the youngest heavyweight boxing champion in history. With unmatched speed and knockout power, he dominated the ring and quickly became a household name. But it wasn't just the wins that piled up; so did the money. At the peak of his career, Tyson earned over $400 million, making him one of the highest-paid athletes in the world.

But there's something even Tyson couldn't dodge: lifestyle creep.

He bought everything: dozens of luxury cars, massive mansions, tigers (yes, actual pet tigers), and even a $2.5 million solid-gold bathtub for his then-wife. He had a full-time staff, bodyguards, entourage, and a spending habit that made headlines.

Eventually, the money stopped flowing in at the same rate. Bad financial decisions piled up. Tyson owed millions in back taxes, unpaid debts, and legal fees. By 2003, he was forced to file for bankruptcy, revealing he was $23 million in debt.[11]

But unlike many celebrities who disappear after a downfall, Tyson did something different. He changed. Tyson took on acting roles and business ventures.

He's now reestablished himself. As of 2024, Tyson's net worth is estimated to be around $10 million, which is not what it once was, but it's a strong comeback given how far he had fallen.[12]

Mike Tyson's story is the perfect reminder that financial success isn't about how much you earn; it's about how you manage what you earn. And if you're smart early, you can avoid the kind of stress even champions face.

11. Jeffrey May, "How Mike Tyson Lost Everything: From $400 Million to Bankrupt 'That's Just How I Lived My Life,'" AS USA, November 5, 2024, https://en.as.com/other_sports/how-mike-tyson-lost-everything-from-400-million-to-bankrupt-thats-just-how-i-lived-my-life-n/.
12. TeeJay Small, "How Mike Tyson Beat Bankruptcy and Came Back with $30m Net Worth," AfroTech, November 19, 2024, https://afrotech.com/mike-tyson-net-worth.

3

The Real Cost Isn't
on the Price Tag

Opportunity cost is one of the most important ideas in personal finance. It's what you *give up* when you make a choice.

It's happening all around you, every single day:

- You stay up late watching YouTube → and give up sleep.
- You buy a new pair of shoes → and give up saving that money.
- You say "yes" to something fun → and say "no" (without realizing it) to something else.

You're trading all the time; it's just that most people don't see the cost behind the choice.

Pool or Popcorn?

You've got two options:

- Go shoot pool with your friends
- Go see the new movie everyone's talking about

You choose pool. It's fun. But then your entire social feed becomes a spoiler zone for the movie. You missed it.

That's opportunity cost: the trade-off behind every choice, even the small ones.

On their own, these moments don't seem like a big deal. But over time, they stack up, especially when they involve your time, money, or future.

Awareness = Power

The goal isn't to cancel fun. It's to protect your freedom.

You *can* spend your money however you want. But every choice has a cost, not just in dollars but also in what you *could've* done with that money.

Max Green Goes to College

Meet Max Green. He's a high school senior trying to figure out what to do next.

Option 1: Start working right away

- $30,000/year salary
- After 4 years: $120,000 earned

Option 2: Go to college

- Tuition and living costs: $25,000/year
- Total college cost: $100,000
- Missed wages: $120,000
- Opportunity Cost of College: $220,000
  (*And that doesn't count the money he could have invested and grown during those years*)

At first glance, working right after high school might seem like the better financial move. You're earning money right away, skipping student debt, and maybe even helping support your family. That's real, and for some people, it's the best option.

But here's the thing: on average, people with college degrees earn significantly more over their lifetimes than those without. According to the APLU, the median earnings for bachelor's degree holders are 84% higher than those with only a high school diploma.[13]

That doesn't mean college is automatically the right choice. It only makes sense if you're getting a good return on your investment. That means choosing a school that won't leave you drowning in debt, picking a major that leads to real job opportunities, and making the most of the college experience, internships, networking, and skill-building included.

In short, opportunity cost helps Max see the *whole* picture— not just the price tag.

The Biggest Opportunity Costs in Life

These are some of the most common (and sneaky) trade-offs that can shape your future:

Time

In later chapters, you'll see this clearly: time is your most powerful asset, especially when it comes to making the most of your investments.

Growth

Skipping out on learning something valuable today might cost you a job, a side hustle, or even your dream business. Every time you avoid leveling up, you're giving up the chance to earn more and live with more freedom later.

Comparison

One of the biggest invisible costs is trying to keep up with people, especially online. You see the shoes, the trips, the setups, but not the debt, stress, or credit card bills behind the scenes. If you're

---

13. "How Does a College Degree Improve Graduates' Employment and Earnings Potential?" APLU, July 31, 2024, https://www.aplu.org/our-work/4-policy-and-advocacy/publicuvalues/employment-earnings/.

chasing someone else's lifestyle, the cost isn't just financial; it's your own goals getting left behind.

Mental Energy

Making too many small, low-value decisions each day drains your brain, as well as the brain rot from endless scrolling and excessive consumption of low-quality content. The opportunity cost? Less focus and creativity for the stuff that actually moves your life forward.

The Baker Purchase Factor: Why That $1,000 TV Really Costs You $1,400

You've probably never heard of the **Baker Purchase Factor**, because we made it up. But once you understand it, you'll never look at money the same way again.

Here's the idea:

When you buy something, you're not just handing over the amount you see on the price tag. You're actually spending money that's already been reduced by taxes—*after-tax money.*

Before that money even reaches your wallet or bank account, a chunk of it is taken out for things like federal taxes, state taxes, and other deductions.

That means to have enough money to buy something, you have to earn even more than the price you see. In other words, every purchase costs you more time, effort, and work than you realize.

When you understand the real cost behind your spending, you start to think a lot smarter about what's worth your money and what's not.

Enter: The Magic Multiplier → 1.4

Let's say you're eyeing a giant 75" TV for $1,000. You've got the money saved up. Great! But hold up . . .

If you had to earn that money at a job, it's not just $1,000 you needed to make.

Why? Taxes.

Let's say your future tax rate is around 28% (pretty average for many adults). That means: You only keep 72% of what you earn (because 100% − 28% = 72%).

To figure out how much you have to earn in order to take home $1, you divide $1 by 0.72:

$$\$1 \div 0.72 = \$1.39$$

Rounding: For every $1 you take home, you have to earn about $1.40. So that $1,000 TV? It really cost you about $1,400 in earnings before taxes.

Boom. That's the **Baker Purchase Factor** in action.

What This Means for You (Even Now)

Even if you're not paying taxes yet, this is your future. And it's good to get in the habit of thinking: "How many hours of work is this *really* going to cost me?"

Examples

Item	Sticker Price	Real Cost (x1.4)
New hoodie	$60	$84
Game console	$500	$700
Sneakers	$150	$210
Concert ticket	$120	$168
Uber Eats every weekend for a month	$200	$280

And if you work a part-time job at $15/hour?

That $500 console = about 47 hours of work.

I'm not saying "never buy fun stuff." But when you *do*, know what it actually costs you.

You're not just spending money; you're spending time, energy, effort, and *taxed income*.

LEVEL UP

Use your notebook or journal for this one. Let's put your money decisions under the microscope.

Pick one thing you *want* to buy soon—maybe something over $100.

    Item I want: _____

    Sticker price: $_____

Multiply it by 1.4 to see the real cost (after taxes).

    Real cost: $_____

Divide that cost by what you make an hour. (If you don't work, divide by your state's minimum wage)

    Hours I'd need to work: _____ hours

Still want it? That's cool—just make it a *choice*, not a surprise, regret, or snap decision.

ONE SMART SWAP

Think of one time this week you could trade a "want" for a better long-term move (like saving, investing, or learning something new).

This week, I will swap: _____

for: _____

That's how you take control of your money and your future.

A WORD FROM

JOE BAKER

From the very beginning, my wife and I made one simple family rule when it came to eating out:

At restaurants, we all drink water. No sodas. No sweet tea. Just water.

Why? Because every dollar we saved skipping pricey drinks was a dollar we could put toward a bigger goal: paying for our daughters' college education. This wasn't just a suggestion, it became *the rule*.

One night when our girls were about 3 and 5 years old, we went out to eat at a local restaurant. When the waiter came by and asked the classic, "What would you like to drink?" my oldest daughter piped up proudly: "I want water because I want to go to college!"

Without missing a beat, her little sister chimed in with her own toddler version: "Me want water! Wanna go college!" The waiter just stood there, a little confused. I didn't even try to explain—it would have taken way too long.

Fast forward to today: Even though we could easily afford any drink on the menu now, we still stick with water out of habit. (And bonus: it's free *and* it's actually good for you.)

Let's do the math:

- 4 people x 3 meals out per week = 12 drinks/week
- $2 drinks = $24/week
- $24/week = $1,248/year

If we invested that $24/week in a low-cost index fund with 8% growth:

- → After 10 years = $18,000
- → After 17 years = $42,000
- → After 30 years = $141,000

Small choices add up to big wins over time. That's college money. A sweet ride. Or even retirement savings.

All hiding in the cost of a soda.

4

College:
Dream, Detour, or Deal?

Ask anyone if college is worth it, and you'll probably hear one of three responses:

1. "Of course! You can't get a good job without it."
2. "Not really. Look at all the debt people are drowning in."
3. "It depends."

Spoiler: It depends.

And the key to answering that question? Understanding something called **ROI**.

ROI (Return on Investment) is a simple but powerful idea:

What do you get for what you give?

When it comes to college, you're not just giving your time and energy. You're also giving up *money* and the chance to *earn* money during those years. The goal? To come out of it with a degree that leads to a well-paying, meaningful career.

But if you spend $100,000 on a degree that leads to a $40,000-a-year job, it could take you decades just to break even.

Meanwhile, someone else might spend $20,000 on a trade certification and earn $60,000 in their first year.

It's not about choosing money *over* passion but ignoring financial peace could lock you into decades of stress and limited freedom.

Choosing a Major: Starting Salaries & ROI Insights

Here's a simplified look at how different education paths can play out financially. These are just ballpark estimates, but they show the big picture.

Major / Field	Avg. Starting Salary	ROI Insight
Nursing	$59,000[a]	Recession-resistant and stable. Requires licensure and clinical training. Strong ROI with moderate student debt.
Business Administration	$60,000[b]	Versatile career paths. Income depends on specialization and industry. Often pursued with graduate degrees.
Education	$60,000[b]	Stable job market. Pay varies by state and often requires a teaching credential. May take longer to pay off loans.
English / Liberal Arts / Humanities	Wide Range $50,000[b]	Strong writing and thinking skills, but may require grad school or career pivot (e.g., marketing, law, teaching) for higher income.
Performing Arts	$46,000[c]	Passion-driven field with less financial stability. May require multiple jobs or freelance work.
Trade School (e.g., HVAC, Plumbing, Welding)	$67,000[d]	Fast entry into the workforce, lower cost to train. Certifications required, but often no 4-year degree. Strong ROI potential.
Psychology	$54,000[e]	Often requires a master's or doctorate for high-paying roles. Good for counseling or therapy but slower financial return.

Major / Field	Avg. Starting Salary	ROI Insight
Marketing / Communications	$55,000[b]	Creative and strategic career paths. Wide salary range depending on industry and experience. Internships help a lot.
Engineering	$73,000[b]	High earning potential and job demand. Requires strong math/science and a 4-year degree (at minimum).
Criminal Justice	$35,000–60,000[f]	Careers in law enforcement or legal systems. May require academy training or further education. Moderate ROI.
Information Technology (IT)	$52,000[g]	Tech-focused field with certifications sometimes replacing full degrees. High growth potential.
Finance / Accounting	$66,000[h]	Good starting salary with room to grow. Often leads to stable, high-paying careers, and a CPA license can boost earnings.

[a] See https://www.indeed.com/career/licensed-practical-nurse/salaries
[b] See https://www.indeed.com/career-advice/pay-salary/average-salary-for-college-graduates
[c] See https://www.salary.com/research/salary/hiring/performing-arts-salary
[d] See https://research.com/careers/best-jobs-for-trade-school-graduates
[e] See https://psychologyjobs.com/career-advice/clinical-psychologist-salary
[f] See https://onlinedegrees.kent.edu/blog/careers-and-salaries
[g] See https://www.indeed.com/career/information-technology-specialist/salaries
[h] See https://www.indeed.com/career/accountant/salaries

Want to explore more careers and compare salaries? Check out the Occupational Outlook Handbook at the U.S. Bureau of Labor Statistics. It's a free government site that shows you how much jobs pay, what training they need, and which fields are growing or shrinking.[1]

Understanding ROI is huge when it comes to choosing a major that fits your goals, budget, and future lifestyle. It helps

1. "Fastest Growing Occupations," U.S. Bureau of Labor Statistics, April 18, 2025, https://www.bls.gov/ooh/fastest-growing.htm.

you think beyond "what sounds fun" and start connecting your interests with real-world outcomes.

College Isn't the Only Path Anymore

Sometimes it feels like high school only shows one path after graduation: go straight to a prestigious 4-year university. But that's no longer the only option, or even the best one for everyone. More and more young people are finding smarter, faster, and more affordable ways to build successful futures.

Here are a few different paths to consider:

Trade Schools[2]

- Fast-track to well-paying jobs like electricians, HVAC techs, mechanics, dental hygienists.
- Often overlooked, but some trades pay more than some degrees.

Apprenticeships[3]

- Learn while you earn. No debt, real-world skills, and a paycheck on day one.
- Available in trades, tech, and even finance or healthcare in some states.

Public Service Programs

- Programs like AmeriCorps, Peace Corps, Conservation Corps, YouthBuild, or Public Health Corps offer experience, pay, and sometimes student loan assistance or scholarships.

2. Thomas Broderick, "The Ultimate Guide to Trade and Vocational Schools," Accredited Schools Online, September 15, 2023, https://www.accreditedschoolsonline.org/vocational-trade-school.
3. For current apprenticeship openings, see https://www.apprenticeship.gov/career-seekers.

Entrepreneurship (with a Plan)
- Start small: lawn care, tutoring, custom clothing, digital design.
- Learn budgeting, marketing, taxes—real-life financial literacy in action.

Online Degrees and Certifications[4]
- Cheaper, more flexible, and increasingly respected.
- Great for tech fields, business, and even healthcare admin.

Gap Year (With Intention)[5]
- Work, travel, volunteer—*but make it count.*
- Can build maturity, gain insight into the work world, help to solidify career decisions, and help avoid wasting time/money on a random major.[6]

Military + GI Bill: More Than Just Boots on the Ground[7]

Serve your country, gain skills, and get your education paid for. The military isn't just about being on the front lines. Sure, there are soldiers, but the military also needs:

- Doctors
- Dentists
- Engineers
- Cybersecurity experts
- Mechanics
- Musicians
- Chefs
- And even video game designers (yes, really—for simulations and training)

---

4. For a list of accredited online colleges, see https://www.usnews.com/education/online-education.
5. For a list of gap year programs in the US, see https://www.gooverseas.com/gap-year/united-states-america.
6. Cole Claybourn, "How a Gap Year Prepares Students for College," USNews, November 29, 2022, https://www.usnews.com/education/best-colleges/articles/what-a-gap-year-is-and-how-it-prepares-students-for-college
7. "GI Bill," Military.com, https://www.military.com/education/gi-bill.

Through the GI Bill, you can get most or all of your college paid for after your service. That means:

- No student debt
- Real-world job experience
- Leadership skills
- Travel (you might see more of the world than most people ever will)
- Free health care
- Matched government contributions in a retirement plan!

> **Important:** The military is a serious commitment that's not for everyone. But for some, it's a powerful way to build a future, gain financial independence, and serve with purpose.

College is one tool, but it's not the only one.

Choosing College

If you do decide to go the college route, there are many options:

Dual Enrollment in High School
- Free or low-cost college credits while still in high school.
- Can graduate college early = save time and money.

Local vs. Out-of-State Universities
- Local: Save tens of thousands by living at home, paying in-state tuition, and working part-time.
- Out-of-State: Sometimes offers unique programs, but comes with higher costs. Make sure it's *worth it*— financially and academically.

Community College First

- 2+2 Plan: Two years at a low-cost community college + two years at a university = same degree for half the price.
- Many offer guaranteed transfer programs.

Apply to College Abroad

Some international universities (especially in Europe and Canada) offer high-quality education for free or a fraction of the US price, and often with shorter degree programs. Hundreds of programs across Europe (especially in the Netherlands, Germany, and Sweden) are taught entirely in English. Many European universities don't require the SAT/ACT. They might consider your high school GPA, AP exam scores, transcripts, and sometimes even a motivation letter or an interview as part of the application process. You'll get to experience a new culture and meet people from all walks of life.

Bonus: Studying abroad can make you stand out to future employers and give you an edge in careers that value global thinking.[8]

College Application Checklist

Applying to college can feel like trying to solve a puzzle . . . blindfolded . . . while someone yells deadlines in your face.

But you've got this. Here's how to break it down:

1. **Make a List of Schools You Like**
   Start by picking 5–10 colleges that seem like a good fit. Don't just chase the "big name" schools. Chase the one that fits you and your goals.

---

8. For a variety of study abroad programs in Europe, see these sites: https://beyondthestates.com; https://www.study-in-germany.com; https://education.ec.europa.eu/study-in-europe; https://www.studyinnl.org

2. **Visit Their Websites**

   Look for the "Admissions" or "Apply Now" section.
   It typically includes application steps, deadlines, and
   requirements. Yes, it's okay to get a little lost at first.

3. **Use the Common App (If You Can)**

   Go to commonapp.org. It lets you apply to hundreds of
   colleges with one application. Super helpful. Saves time.
   Keeps you organized. A total lifesaver.

4. **Request Your Transcript**

   This is your official high school grade history. You don't
   need to send it yourself. Ask your school counselor, and
   they'll handle it.

5. **Write a Personal Statement or Essay**

   This is your chance to show schools who you are
   beyond your GPA. Be honest. Be real. Be you.

6. **Ask for Letters of Recommendation**

   These are written by teachers, counselors, or coaches
   who can hype you up and vouch for your character.
   Ask early, and give them at least 2–3 weeks to write it.
   And remember to say thank you.

7. **Pay the Application Fee (or Get a Waiver)**

   Application fees can be $30–$75 each. Can't swing it?
   Ask your counselor for a fee waiver. It's super common,
   and colleges won't hold it against you.

8. **Submit Everything on Time**

   Set calendar reminders. Write it on your forehead.
   Whatever works. Deadlines matter.

Questions to Ask Before You Commit to College

- [ ] Is this degree required for the job I want?
- [ ] What's the average salary in that field?
- [ ] Will I need grad school to be competitive?
- [ ] How much will I need to borrow, and how long will it take to pay it off?
- [ ] Can I get the same results with a cheaper path?
- [ ] Am I doing this for *me* or because I think I *have* to?

Know the Facts Before You Pick a College

Before you choose a college (or even decide where to apply), check out collegescorecard.ed.gov. It's a free website from the U.S. Department of Education that gives you the real scoop on colleges and majors across the country.

You can find out things like:

- What it really costs to attend each school (after scholarships and financial aid)
- Graduation rates and how many students actually finish
- How much student debt graduates take on
- Admissions test scores and acceptance rates
- Campus diversity and what the student body looks like
- How much money graduates earn after college
- Data to compare fields of study offered at colleges and universities

You can even compare several colleges side by side. No hype, no fluff—just the facts you need to make a smart decision.

Hidden Costs

When people talk about paying for college, most think about **tuition**—the official price to take classes. But the truth is, there's a whole world of hidden costs that can sneak up on you if you're not prepared.

A lot of students are shocked when they realize the true cost of college is way more than just the sticker price. Why? Because it's not just books and classes—it's *everything else* too.

Here are some everyday college costs to keep on your radar[9]:

×   **Books & Class Materials**—Textbooks are pricey. Even digital versions or rentals can cost a lot. Save money by borrowing, renting, or buying used whenever you can.

×   **Transportation**—Whether it's flights home for the holidays or gas for your car, getting around isn't free. Public transit or carpooling might save you big.

×   **Food**—Your school might offer a meal plan, but it won't always cover snacks, coffee runs, or late-night takeout.

×   **Campus Activities**—Joining a club, sports team, or Greek life often comes with fees and dues. These are awesome experiences, but just make sure they fit your budget.

×   **Everyday Life Stuff**—Laundry, toothpaste, cleaning supplies, shampoo—you name it. These little things add up fast when you're living on your own.

×   **Emergency Funds**—Unexpected costs pop up. Maybe your laptop crashes. Maybe you need a last-minute bus ticket or urgent medical care. Having a small emergency stash can be a lifesaver.

×   **Fees**—Schools often charge extra fees that aren't always obvious. These can sneak onto your bill and add up fast if you're not prepared. Some to watch out for are[10]:

    –   *Orientation Fee*—A one-time charge just for attending new student orientation.

9. Elaine Rubin, "Mastering College Finances: Uncovering Hidden Costs Beyond Tuition," Edvisors, May 24, 2024, https://www.edvisors.com/blog/uncovering-hidden-costs-beyond-tuition/.

10. Sarah Wood, "12 college fees that may surprise you | paying for college," U.S. News, May 11, 2023, https://www.usnews.com/education/best-colleges/paying-for-college/articles/college-fees-that-may-surprise-you.

- *Graduation Fee*—Some schools make you pay to apply for graduation or get your diploma.
- *Activity or Athletic Fees*—Helps fund campus events or sports, even if you don't participate.
- *Technology Fee*—Covers Wi-Fi, online platforms, or computer labs.
- *Lab or Course Fees*—Extra costs for science labs, art supplies, or special materials.

A Major Decision

We're not anti-college—we're pro-*you*.

College can absolutely be a game-changer. It can open doors, expand your mind, and connect you to people and opportunities you'd never meet otherwise.

However, know this: If you decide not to go to college, you're far from alone. These days, a significant number of Gen Z and millennials are choosing different paths instead of traditional higher education.[11]

College is one path, not *the only* one. And it's a path that works best when you walk it with your eyes wide open.

Explore every option, from trade schools to gap years, apprenticeships to online learning. Stack up the facts. Use tools to compare costs, earnings, and debt. Look out for the hidden stuff, too, like fees, living costs, and everyday expenses that can quietly drain your budget.

So whether your next step is freshman orientation, launching a business, or wiring your first HVAC unit, just make sure it's *your* decision on your terms and with your future in mind.

In the end, *college is a tool*. The power comes from how you use it. It can be a dream, a detour, or a deal.

It's up to you to decide which one it becomes.

11. Ayelet Sheffey and Juliana Kaplan, "Over Half of Gen Z and Millennials Are Living Paycheck to Paycheck—and College Is One of the First Things They're Cutting from Their Budgets," *Business Insider*, May 15, 2024, https://www.businessinsider.com/gen-z-millennials-skipping-college-living-paycheck-to-paycheck-2024-5.

LEVEL UP

This one's all about facts, not hype. Use your notebook or journal to answer the questions below and start building your own decision blueprint.

What kind of life do you want 5–10 years from now? Think about lifestyle, career, impact, and freedom.

`In 10 years, I want to:` _____

Do you think college is the best next step for that life? Why or why not?

`My take on college right now:` _____

COMPARE TWO PATHS

Pick *one college major* you're considering and *one non-college path* (like a trade, military, online certification, or entrepreneurship).

Path	Starting Salary	Cost to Train	Time to Complete	Job Demand
College	$_____	$_____	_____ years	☐ High ☐ Medium ☐ Low
Non-College	$_____	$_____	_____ years	☐ High ☐ Medium ☐ Low

What surprised you about this comparison?

What's one action you can take this week to move closer to making a decision that's *right for you*—not just expected of you?

`This week, I will:` _____

A WORD FROM
ANTHONY ZAMOR

I grew up attending Kaiserslautern High School on a US military base in Germany, and for most of my life, this country has been home. So when it came time to think about college, I didn't feel the need to go far.

I found Schiller International University thanks to a little help from my family. My grandfather was actually the one who first discovered it while researching schools in Germany. After that, I dug into it more on my own and later came across their booth at the KHS college fair. I spoke with a representative and learned a lot about what they offered. What really stood out to me was that Schiller had campuses not only in Heidelberg but also in Paris, Madrid, and even Tampa, Florida. I liked knowing that I could start in one place and have the option to transfer somewhere else if I wanted.

The application process was incredibly simple. I applied online, submitted my high school transcripts, and waited to hear back. Honestly, it was one of the easiest things I've done in my college journey. From what I've seen, it was very similar to the process most students go through when applying to universities in the US.

So far, the academic experience has been a good fit. All of my classes are taught in English, and Heidelberg is what they call a "student city," which means the whole place is very friendly to university students. There are a lot of people my age here, which makes it easy to meet others and build friendships. I've gotten to connect with people from all over the world, which is something that really appealed to me about studying here. Beyond that, I've also started to understand how the German system works, which is something that I know will help me when I begin my career, whether I stay in Germany or move elsewhere in Europe.

In terms of cost, things are pretty comparable to what students in the US pay, especially when it comes to renting a dorm or small apartment. I don't have access to a dining hall or meal plan, so I do all my own grocery shopping and cooking. That's been a bit of a learning curve. Tuition is definitely cheaper than most private US schools, but it's more expensive than attending a public German university, which is basically free for locals. Thankfully, I received a scholarship that will save me around $16,000 over four years, which really helps.

Adjusting to college life here was actually pretty smooth. I speak fluent German, which gave me a big advantage, especially compared to many of my international classmates who don't speak the language at all. Most of my closest friends are from other countries. And while not all of them speak German, that's part of what makes this place feel so international. The biggest adjustment for me wasn't the country but learning to live on my own. Cooking, managing my schedule, taking care of my space; that part took time, but it's helped me grow a lot.

Would I recommend this route to other American students? Definitely. Studying abroad is one of the best ways to travel, see the world, and connect with different cultures, all while getting your education. It challenges you, opens your mind, and gives you experiences that you just can't get if you stay in one place. For me, studying in Germany wasn't just about earning a degree; it was about building a life I actually want to live.

A WORD FROM
MARK ELLIS

High school programs tend to push college as the default next step, but I knew it wasn't the right path for me. The more I looked into it, the more the numbers stressed me out. I didn't want to spend the next ten, twenty years drowning in student loan debt just to get a degree I might not use. So I started seeking an alternative.

One day after school, I talked to my uncle who's a licensed master electrician. He told me that he actually made about

$84,000 a year, with no college degree and no student debt. That conversation flipped a switch for me. I started researching trade schools and apprenticeships in my area, and I found out there were real options that could lead to solid careers.

Instead of applying to colleges, I applied to a local union electrical apprenticeship program. It was a five-year program that included both paid on-the-job training and classroom instruction. I had to submit my high school transcript, take a basic math and reading exam, and do an interview. I didn't need a 4.0 GPA or SAT score. They primarily wanted to know if I could show up, learn, and work hard.

I got accepted and started a few months after graduation. In my first year, I was already earning around $16/hour, working full time while attending classes a couple nights a week. Each year, my pay went up as I gained more skills and experience. Now, two years after finishing my apprenticeship, I'm earning about $52,000 a year, plus full benefits, and I love what I do.

I work with my hands, I solve real problems every day, and I'm proud of the projects I work on. It feels good to know my work matters.

Some of my friends went to college, and that worked for them. But for me, the trades were the right fit. No debt. Solid income. A job that's in demand. And I can even start my own business one day.

If I could give any advice to someone unsure about college, it's this: Look at what fits your strengths, your goals, and your future. There is not a one-size-fits-all.

5

Launch Your Career

When you think about "getting a job," you might picture this:

A stiff shirt. A resume printed on fancy paper.

A sweaty handshake in a beige office.

A swivel chair under flickering fluorescent lights.

A manager who says, "Let me circle back."

A 9-to-5 grind where you watch the clock more than you watch your goals.

Work. Eat. Sleep. Repeat.

Climb the ladder.

Wait for the promotion.

Stick with one company for 40 years.

Retire.

Collect a pension.

Wait . . . that was the old world.

It's a new era. An era where you can start a business from your phone. You can freelance, gig, or go remote. You may jump from one career field to another. Your skills matter more than your degree.

The rules have changed. The opportunities have exploded.

Your future career isn't something you land; it's something you launch.

Let's break down the new game plan for getting started: skills, power moves, and how to make decisions today that pay off tomorrow.

Networking: Your Hidden Superpower

No matter how much the job world changes, one thing stays the same: Relationships are everything.

> "Your network is your net worth."
> —Porter Gale

Networking isn't about using people. It's about building genuine relationships with people who can:

- Teach you
- Encourage you
- Open doors for you
- Challenge you
- Inspire you

It's not about what people can *give* you today. It's about growing together, so that when opportunities show up, you're already in the room.

Networking Future-Focused Tips:

→ **Stay curious:** Ask people about their careers, their journeys, their advice.
→ **Stay grateful:** Always thank people who share their time or wisdom.
→ **Stay visible:** Update your LinkedIn. Share your projects. Be active in communities related to your interests.
→ **Stay generous:** Share interesting articles, encourage others, offer your skills when you can.

Networking is planting seeds today for a future you can't even imagine yet.

How to Apply for Jobs (The Smart, Professional Way)

Even in a world full of tech, the basics of applying still matter. But you can work smarter, not harder.

Here's your checklist:

☐ *Have a Clean, Sharp Résumé*

- A quick snapshot of who you are professionally (skills, experiences, achievements)
- Keep it to one page
- Focus on achievements, not just duties ("Increased social media engagement by 40%" vs. "Managed Instagram account")
- *Customize it for each job*

☐ *Write a Cover Letter*

- A short, specific letter that shows *why* you want the job and *why* you're a great fit
- Focus on them, not you ("What can I bring to your team?")

☐ *Create a Professional Online Profile*

- LinkedIn is a must, even as a student or recent grad
- Share your story: internships, projects, certifications, even volunteer work
- Include a professional-looking photo (clear, friendly, real, but not a selfie at a concert)

☐ *Use Online Tools*

- **Canva**—free templates for resumes

- **Resume.io**—builds strong resumes and cover letters
- **Grammarly**—cleans up your writing
- **AI**—help drafting cover letters, prepping interview answers (but *always* edit it to sound like you)

☐ *Prepare References*

- Ask teachers, former bosses, or mentors ahead of time
- Choose people who will speak highly of your work ethic and character
- Keep copies of reference letters for future applications.

☐ *Practice Interview Skills*

- Use common interview questions
- Record yourself practicing (yes, it feels weird—but it works!)

> **Tip:** Keep all your application materials including custom résumés, cover letters, reference letters, certificates, etc. in one well-organized folder on your Google Drive. You never know what you'll need for future opportunities, and having everything in one place will save you time, stress, and last-minute scrambling.

Customize!

You should customize your cover letter and résumé for each application. Every. Single. Time.

Imagine showing up to 10 different birthday parties: a pool party, a fancy dinner, a backyard bonfire, and wearing the exact same outfit and giving the same card and gift.

Nobody's impressed. It feels off. It's like you didn't even try to match the moment.

That's what sending the same resume and cover letter to every job is like. It's not thoughtful. It doesn't fit. And the companies can tell when it is a mass message.

Want to know a smart way to get noticed? Speak their language. Use *their* words, literally.

When you're writing your résumé or cover letter, look at the job posting or the company's website. Pay attention to the exact words and phrases they use. Are they looking for someone who's "creative," "detail-oriented," or "a team player"? Do they describe their workplace as "fast-paced" or "driven by purpose"?

Now take some of those same words and weave them into your own writing—honestly, of course.

Why? Because imitation is the sincerest form of flattery, and it also shows you get them. You're showing that you're not just applying to any job. You're applying to this one, because you read, listened, and understood what they care about.

It's like when you're trying to join a new group or team. You don't come in talking about stuff no one relates to.

You show you know the vibe. You match their energy.

So Why Customize?

- It shows you actually care.
  - They can tell you didn't just copy and paste the same thing for every job.

- You stand out from lazy applicants.
  - Most people don't bother customizing. You do, so you get noticed.

- You can highlight what they are looking for.
  - If the job says they want someone who's great with people, then you tell a story that proves it.

- You make it easy for them to say yes.
  - When they see "Wow, this person fits what we need," it's an easy decision.

The Art of Face-to-Face (Even When Applying Online)

In a digital world, face-to-face skills are rare and powerful. Even if you apply online, find ways to create real human connections.

Some ideas:

- Visit the business if you can.
- Meet someone from the company at an event or fair.
- Send a thank-you note (yes, old-school) after an interview.
- Smile and make eye contact during Zoom calls.
- Follow up politely, showing enthusiasm.

People hire people they like, not just people who tick the boxes. In a sea of online applicants, the person who feels real will always have the advantage.

Your Career Is Something You Build— Not Something You Find

Your future isn't waiting for you to stumble into it. It's something you build, day by day, skill by skill, relationship by relationship.

The sooner you start, the sooner you launch.

Your career isn't a straight path; it's a creative space. It's where you experiment, explore, build, and launch. You're not just walking it—you're designing it. And the best part? You get to keep evolving as you go.

LEVEL UP

Time to stop waiting and start building. Your future career isn't going to fall into your lap; you've got to *launch it*.

In your journal write down 3 skills you already have that could help you earn money, land a job, or build something cool.

If someone Googled you today, what would they see?

Choose one of the following to either create or clean up this week:

- ☐ **Start or update your LinkedIn profile**
- ☐ **Organize your résumé in Google Drive**
- ☐ **Clean up social media posts that don't reflect who you are**

NETWORK MOVE OF THE WEEK

Relationships open doors. Practice writing a short thank-you note to someone who has helped you, and *actually* give it to them.

A WORD FROM

KRISTEN BELEW

One of the most unexpected opportunities came from something as simple as writing a thank-you note.

During college, I took a leadership course taught by the president of the university. At the end of the semester, I sent him a short thank-you letter, just to say how much I appreciated the class and what I learned.

Not long after, he nominated me to attend a statewide Student Leadership Forum—a three-day event bringing together student leaders from universities across the state. It was a chance to meet new people, grow in leadership, and hear from inspiring speakers.

Again, I followed up with a thank-you note, this time to the director of the forum. I wasn't expecting anything in return. I just wanted to show gratitude.

Months later, I got a surprise email. Because of that note and the connection it built, I was invited to an all-expenses-paid trip to Washington, D.C., to attend the National Prayer Breakfast and the National Student Leadership Forum. For three days, I was surrounded by passionate, purpose-driven students from around the world. We listened to global leaders, including the President of the United States, the Speaker of the House, and even a well-known college football quarterback who, at the time, just happened to be my college crush.

Thank-you notes matter. They open doors, show character, and help you stand out in a world where most people just move on. A simple act of kindness and respect can lead to opportunities you never saw coming.

A WORD FROM
CAMILA MORALES

I graduated right after the 2008 housing crisis and recession, and it wasn't exactly the dream economy you hope to walk into.

Jobs were scarce, companies were laying people off left and right, and I was getting desperate. I had submitted countless online applications . . . and heard nothing back. Not even a rejection email most of the time.

It felt like I was shouting into a void. So I decided to try something different.

Instead of just applying online and waiting, I printed out stacks of my resumes and cover letters and started showing up in person.

I walked into businesses, even places that didn't have "Help Wanted" signs, and asked if there was anyone available to talk to.

If there was, I handed them my resume personally.

If there wasn't, I left it with a smile and a thank you.

It wasn't glamorous.

It wasn't easy.

But it worked.

Turns out, actually showing up, shaking a hand, and making a quick impression set me apart from the hundreds of people applying online.

Face-to-face still mattered. And it gave me opportunities I wouldn't have gotten otherwise.

A WORD FROM

HEATHER HEWITT

At the time, I was working as an activities director at a retirement center, and honestly, I loved it. The work was meaningful, the people were amazing, and every day felt like I was making a real difference.

But even though I was happy, I always kept my eyes and ears open.

Maybe something would come along with better hours.

Maybe a position with more chances for growth.

Maybe even a little more pay.

I wasn't desperately job hunting, but I was *prepared* if the right opportunity showed up.

Sometimes I would attend random community events, even when I didn't know a single person who would be there. You never know, right?

One evening, I stumbled across what looked like a Chamber of Commerce event downtown.

Honestly, I didn't even know if it was open to the public.

But I thought, *Why not?* and walked in anyway.

I started mingling, introducing myself, asking people what they did, just making conversation. And guess what? One of the people I talked to mentioned they were hiring and invited me to come in for an interview.

I didn't even know exactly *what* the job was, but polishing your interview skills is never a bad idea, right? Showing up, staying curious, and taking that small risk opened a door I never would've found otherwise.

And it all started just by being willing to walk into a room full of strangers.

6

No Trust Fund?
No Problem.

What if I told you that you could become a millionaire, even if you never earn six figures, never win the lottery, and never go viral on TikTok?

Sounds fake, right? But it's *real*. In fact, there are nearly 22 million people with a net worth of over one million US dollars in the United States.[1]

And no, they're not all celebrities, CEOs, or crypto bros. Most of them are regular people, doing regular jobs . . . with *exceptional habits*.

What *Is* a Millionaire, Really?

Let's break it down:

× A millionaire isn't someone who *makes* a million dollars a year.

→ A millionaire is someone whose **net worth** is $1,000,000 or more.

Here's the formula:

Assets − Liabilities = Net Worth

1. Einar H. Dyvik, "Countries with the Most Affluent People 2023," Statista, February 18, 2025, https://www.statista.com/statistics/268411/countries-with-the-most-millionaires/.

→ **Assets** = things you own that have value (like cash, investments, retirement accounts, cars, or houses)

→ **Liabilities** = what you owe (like student loans, credit card debt, or car loans)

So yes, even your used Honda or small business counts as part of your net worth.

And we especially like to zoom in on your **liquid net assets**. That's your money that you can access now, like savings, investments, and retirement funds. That's the kind of wealth that gives you real options.

Starting at zero is actually a strong place to begin, because it means you don't owe more than you own. You don't have a negative net worth. One of the greatest roadblocks to building wealth is debt, so avoiding it or paying it down early gives you a huge advantage.

Millionaire Myths: Busted

Let's clear the air. You don't have to be rich, lucky, or brilliant to become a millionaire. You just need *a plan*.

According to a national study[2]:

- 79% of millionaires received zero inheritance
- 8 in 10 invested regularly in a 401(k)
- Only 31% ever made over $100k in a single year
- 1 in 3 never made six figures—ever
- Top 5 careers? Engineer, accountant, teacher, manager, attorney

2. Ramsey Solutions, "The National Study of Millionaires," Ramsey Solutions, Accessed May 7, 2025, https://www.ramseysolutions.com/retirement/the-national-study-of-millionaires-research.

The Millionaire Next Door (Still Exists)

Imagine your neighbor across the street. Drives a beat-up truck. Paid off their house early. Doesn't post about money online.

That person might be a millionaire.

Two researchers studied real millionaires for 20+ years and wrote about it in *The Millionaire Next Door.*[3]

Here's what they found:

- They were self-employed, frugal, and disciplined.
- They managed the budget like a CFO (Chief Financial Officer).
- They invested *consistently*, not aggressively.
- They lived *well below* their means.

And now? That quiet millionaire might be:

- A freelance graphic designer with no debt
- A public school teacher with a Roth IRA
- A couple who never upgraded their car, but invested every month

Want to Build Wealth? Start Here.

You don't need:

- ✕ A huge salary
- ✕ A rich family
- ✕ A business that blows up overnight

You need a plan and the patience to stick with it. Here's how to start today:

Step 1: Open a Starter Money Account (See chapter 13)

Even if it's just $10/month. Habits beat hype.

---

3. Thomas J. Stanley, William D. Danko, and Sarah Stanley Fallaw, *The Millionaire Next Door: The Surprising Secrets of America's Wealthy* (Lanham: Taylor Trade Publishing, 2016).

Step 2: Track Your Money (See chapter 9)

Know where it goes. Don't let your cash disappear without a trace.

Step 3: Learn One Money Skill Each Month (See chapter 16)

You've got the tools to build wealth one smart move at a time.

Millionaire status isn't about being born into money.

It's about making consistent, intentional moves that your future self will thank you for.

LEVEL UP

Forget the myths. Wealth isn't about luck. It's about habits. Let's start yours today.

KNOW YOUR NET WORTH (EVEN IF IT'S $0)

Start by writing down what you *own* and what you *owe*. Don't worry if it's not much—this is just your starting line.

Things I own with value (cash, savings, car, etc.):
What I owe (loans, credit cards, etc.):
My current net worth:

YOUR FIRST MILLIONAIRE HABIT

Pick one of these small but powerful habits to start this week:

☐ Track every dollar I spend

☐ Start saving even $5–10 per week

☐ Read or watch a video about investing basics

☐ Open a savings account

This week, I will: _____

A WORD FROM
JASON REECE

This is the story of how my financial life got completely flipped, turned upside down. It's how I went from eating free chips and salsa for dinner to becoming a millionaire by 33 years old. But more importantly, it's the story of how I learned that money is about more than just stacking up dollars. It's about finding real balance in life.

I grew up in South Carolina with parents who were the definition of frugal (like, "reuse the same gift bags for 10 years" kind of frugal). At home, money was treated like a limited resource, and every dollar had a job.

I knew early on that I wanted a career that paid well. The problem? It's hard to know what you want to be when you're still figuring out who you are. And I wasn't exactly killing it in high school. I graduated with a rock-solid 2.7 GPA. My dream school, the University of South Carolina, sent me a "thanks but no thanks" letter. So I pivoted, enrolled in a smaller college, and decided to treat high school as practice and college as game time.

Freshman year, I turned it ON—pulling a 3.9 GPA, getting recognized for academic achievement, and even getting inducted into the Freshman Honor Society. That work paid off, literally. I transferred to the University of South Carolina with an academic scholarship, double majored in Management and Marketing, and started working side hustles and learning to invest (even though my first attempts at stock trading were, let's just say, "learning experiences").

Fast forward: for the last nine years, I focused on climbing the corporate ladder at a company worth nearly $400 billion. Thanks to working hard, investing consistently, and, just as important, spending smartly, I became a liquid millionaire by the age of 33.

But here's the thing: Growing up frugal made me really good at saving money . . . sometimes *too* good. I realized that hoarding money and missing out on experiences was the exact opposite of the full life I wanted. I made a decision: I wouldn't just save. I would also live.

Today, my money mindset is a hybrid—part boomer, part millennial, all about balance:

→ Smartly save, but also spend on the experiences that make life unforgettable.
→ Work hard and do quality work, but don't work yourself into the ground.
→ Be a positive force in the world, but find what actually makes you happy.

7

What Is the Cheat Code?

Back in the day, before smartphones ruled the world, there were a couple of magical words that unlocked infinite wealth in the computer game *The Sims*. A millennial would likely still remember one: Rosebud;!;!;!;!

A couple taps of the keyboard and BOOM! Your Sim had more money than you knew what to do with. No job. No bills. Just endless furniture upgrades and zero consequences.

Unfortunately, real life doesn't come with cheat codes . . . or does it?

Okay, you can't type in a code and become a millionaire. But there are real-life "cheat codes" to getting ahead. This chapter is here to hand you those codes. No controller required.

Imagine this: You're 18 years old and someone offers you a choice.

- Option 1: Take $10,000 right now.
- Option 2: Wait until you're 65, and get $100,000 instead.

Which would you choose?

Wouldn't you go for the $100,000? It sounds like a no-brainer compared to just $10,000. Well, here's the thing: If you took option 1 and invested that $10k instead of spending it, letting it grow with **compound interest** over time, you could have way more than $100k by age 65, without ever adding another dollar.

That's the power of the **Time Value of Money**.

It's not just about how much you have; it's about when you start using it wisely. Every dollar you invest early is like planting a seed. Give it enough time, and it grows into something massive. That's how small money becomes big money—not overnight, but over time.

The **Time Value of Money** is the idea that money you have today is worth more than the same amount in the future.

Because money now can be saved, invested, and used to grow.

And money later? It's losing power while you wait.

There is another reason why NOW is the correct answer.

As time goes on, money doesn't buy as much because of something called **inflation.**

Inflation is the rise in prices over time, which means your money buys less than it used to.

Once upon a time, a penny could actually buy something. A gumball. A piece of candy. Maybe even a phone call (ask your grandparents). Today? A penny can't even cover the sales tax on a stick of gum.

And here's the wild part: it now costs the government more than a penny to make a single penny.[1] Because of this, the US Treasury plans to phase it out of production. So not only is it basically worthless in your pocket, but it's literally worth *less* than it used to be.

That's inflation in action.

But here's the twist: those "worthless" pennies can still matter—if you give them a job to do.

Put those coins (or dollars) into investments that grow faster than inflation, and they don't just hold their value; they increase it. That's how your future self gets ahead.

---

1. "How much does it cost to produce coins?" GovMint, August 18, 2024, https://www.govmint.com/coin-authority/post/how-much-does-it-cost-to-produce-coins?.

So, yes, a penny might be small. But when you understand how inflation works, you'll see why using money wisely now can save you from falling behind later.[2]

What Is Compound Interest?

Here's where the magic happens.

Compound interest is when you earn money on the money you saved *and* on the money that your savings already earned.

Imagine you get a coin in a game, and every 10 seconds, it duplicates itself: 1 coin becomes 2, then 4, then 8, then 16 . . . That's compound growth. It starts slow, then snowballs. It's your cash in beast mode.

So what's the move?

Start investing early. Stay consistent.

Let time do the heavy lifting.

Let's Meet Three Savers

Take a look at the chart below that shows **compound interest** in action from three people, with the same amount saved, but very different outcomes due to the time factor.

Name	Age When They Saved	Amount Invested	Balance at Age 60
Jada Early	25–35	$30,000	$297,635
Marcus Middle	35–45	$30,000	$151,511
Tina Late	45–55	$30,000	$68,140

All three invested $250 per month for 10 years, totaling $30,000 each, and assuming an 8% annual (yearly) return compounded monthly.

Same amount. Same monthly deposit.

2. For a quick measure of inflation rates over time, see https://www.usinflationcalculator.com.

The only difference? *Time.*

Jada started earlier, and she ended up with more than four times what Tina had.

That's the power of starting young.

Not more money; just more time.

A Quick Word on *Negative* Compound Interest

This whole concept works in reverse too. **Cue the groans**

If you have debt, like a credit card, and you carry a balance, compound interest starts working against you. Just like with investing, you're paying interest on the original amount plus the interest that keeps stacking up over time.

Only this time, instead of building your future, it's quietly draining your bank account.

Let's say you have a $500 balance on a credit card with a 20% interest rate. If you only make the minimum payment each month, you could end up paying hundreds of extra dollars in interest, and it could take years to pay off something that started as a single shopping trip.

Why? Because that interest doesn't just sit still. It multiplies. Have you ever seen *The Gremlins*? One turns into ten real quick, especially if you feed it.

Use compound interest to build wealth, not build debt. The same powerful force that can grow your savings can also trap you if you're not paying attention.

A Final Word

You don't have to be rich to invest. You just have to start sooner.

You don't need to wear a suit or read *The Wall Street Journal* to build wealth. You don't have to be some hedge fund genius in New York or a Silicon Valley tech bro with millions. Some of the smartest investors? They're regular people who simply started early and stayed consistent, whether it was through a simple app, a retirement account, or even investing in their own skills.

Most adults don't even start thinking about investing until their 30s. But you? You're ahead of the curve.

That means you have the most powerful advantage of all.

Because when it comes to money . . .

TIME is the cheat code.

And the best time to start building with it?

Now.

LEVEL UP

You just learned the most powerful wealth-building move in the game—starting early. Now it's time to use it. Pick up your journal for the following:

Pick one of these actions that your future self will thank you for:

☐ **Open a savings or investing app**

☐ **Talk to an adult about how they save or invest**

☐ **Watch a short video on compound interest**

☐ **Write down one big goal you'd love to fund in the future (travel, house, business, etc.)**

This week, I will: _____

If you invested just $25 a month starting now, how much could that grow into by the time you're 60? Use a free online compound interest calculator like the one at Investor.gov. Use between 5–8% interest rate.

Try it out and write your result here:

My future total: $_____

(Just from $25/month!)

JASON REECE

Albert Einstein, yeah, the Einstein, once called compound interest "the 8th wonder of the world." He said, "He who understands it, earns it. He who doesn't, pays it."

Thanks to my dad, who was basically a walking personal finance manual, I got introduced to this stuff way earlier than most people. How early? At 14 years old, I was sitting in the front seat of my dad's truck, picking investment funds for my very first 401(k). Yeah, you read that right, 14!

The biggest "lightbulb moment" came a few years later, when I was in college. Every month, my dad would actually mail (yes, old-school, paper mail) me these newsletters from the company managing my 401(k).

One newsletter changed everything. It explained compound interest using simple charts: One chart showed how a tiny investment could turn into a huge pile of money over time. Another showed how spending money today instead of investing it could cost you thousands—or even hundreds of thousands—later.

It hit me: Every $5 coffee. Every random online shopping spree. Every fast food run. It wasn't just costing me today; it was costing Future Me big time.

Spending $50 today could be losing $500 (or more) later.

That's when compound interest went from a boring textbook idea to a superpower I actually understood. You don't need a lot of money to get started. You need time. And you already have it. Start early. Stay consistent. Let compound interest do the heavy lifting.

I was working part time for our family's construction company, which meant I somehow qualified for a retirement plan before I could even drive. Confused and a little overwhelmed, I asked my dad: "What did Matt (my brother) pick for his funds?" Without missing a beat, my dad, who didn't hand out a lot of soft answers, said: "Don't worry about what Matt picked."

That one sentence ended up teaching me more about money, and life, than I realized at the time: Your financial future is your own responsibility.

8

Where to Put Your
First Paycheck

If you're reading this, you're about to become the boss of your own money. And guess what? It all starts with opening your first bank account. It's easier than you think, and it's way cooler than hiding cash in your sock drawer.

First, find a bank or credit union that makes sense for you. Look for places with no fees for students, strong mobile apps, and lots of nearby ATMs. Some even give you rewards just for saving!

To open your account, you'll need a photo ID, your Social Security number, proof of address, and a little bit of starting money (even $25 is fine!). You can set it up online or in person, and it usually doesn't take long. Before you leave, make sure to download the bank's app, set up your online account, and turn on extra security features like multi-factor authentication.

Why a Bank Account Is a Game-Changer

Having a bank account keeps your money safer than carrying cash. It also makes getting paid from jobs way easier with **direct deposit**. Plus, your savings can grow over time by earning a little bit of extra cash called interest. Building good money habits now makes adulting later (like renting apartments, traveling, or buying cars) a whole lot easier.

Checking vs. Savings: What's the Deal?

Your **checking account** is like your money's "hangout spot." It's where your money comes in and goes out for everyday stuff, like snacks, gas, movies—you name it. It comes with a debit card, which lets you spend your own money directly.

Your **savings account** is like your money's "safe house." It's a place to park cash you don't plan to touch right away. And bonus: it earns a little extra money (called **interest**) just for sitting there. Some banks even help by automatically moving money from checking to savings, which makes saving feel almost effortless.

But there are some drawbacks. Standard savings accounts at big banks usually offer *tiny* **interest** rates; sometimes so small you'd earn less than a dollar a year on $1,000. That's not exactly wealth-building.

Also, if you leave *too much* money just sitting there, you're actually losing value over time thanks to **inflation**. (That's when prices go up, but your money doesn't.) So while it's smart to have a savings buffer, it's not the best place for long-term growth. This would be the best place to keep your emergency fund, which we will talk about later.

Not all savings accounts are created equal.

There's a special type of account called a **high-yield savings account**. It works just like a regular savings account, but it pays you more interest.

While your average savings account at a big bank might earn you a tiny amount (like 0.01% interest), a high-yield savings account could earn you 10 to 20 times more. That means your money grows faster just by sitting there!

These accounts are often offered by online banks or credit unions that don't have the same overhead costs as traditional banks, which is how they're able to pay you more.

You can still access your money, just like with a regular savings account, but you'll get a much better return over time.

Debit vs. Credit

When you swipe a **debit card**, you're spending money you already have in your bank account. It keeps you from overspending and is great for building smart habits.

A **credit card** lets you borrow money you'll have to pay back later, and if you're not careful, it's easy to fall into debt. Used wisely, credit cards can help you build a strong credit score, but for now, focus on mastering your debit card first.

Opening a Bank Account

Seriously, no one wants to stand in a long bank line or fill out a pile of paperwork just to open a checking account. The good news? You don't have to.

Thanks to online banking, you can open an account straight from your phone or laptop in under 15 minutes. No suits, no awkward conversations. Just a few taps and you're in.

Here's How It Works

1. **Online Banks** (like Chime, Ally, or Current)
    –   You can open and manage your account completely online. No physical bank branches, no in-person anything. These apps are built for mobile-first, real-time banking.

2. **Traditional Banks with Online Options**
    (like Capital One or Chase)
    –   Even major banks now let you open accounts online. Fill out a form, upload your ID, link your info, and boom, you're ready to go.

What You'll Need to Open an Account

- ☐ A government-issued photo ID (like a driver's license or state ID)
- ☐ Your Social Security number (used for tax and identity purposes)
- ☐ A home or mailing address
- ☐ A small deposit in form of a check or direct deposit from your job works (some banks require $10–$25, but many let you start with $0)

Under 18? You might need a parent or guardian to help open a joint or teen account. Some platforms, like Fidelity Youth, Capital One's teen account, or Chase First Banking, make the process easy with parent-friendly tools.

What to Look for in a Banking App

You want a bank that's easy to use and doesn't sneak in fees. Look for:

- ☐ No monthly fees
- ☐ No minimum balance requirements
- ☐ An app that's clean, simple, and fast
- ☐ FDIC insurance (so your money is protected up to $250,000)
- ☐ Real-time alerts to help you stay on top of your money
- ☐ Free transfers and ATM access

Top User-Friendly Online Banks and Apps[1]

Chime

- No monthly or overdraft fees
- Earlier access to your paycheck
- Checking and savings included

---

1. Sophia Acevedo, "Best Mobile Banking Apps for May 2025," Business Insider, April 29, 2025, https://www.businessinsider.com/personal-finance/banking/best-mobile-banking-apps.

- Clean app with helpful spending alerts

Capital One 360
- No-fee checking and savings
- Great mobile app and customer support
- Has physical branches if you ever want in-person help

Ally Bank
- No monthly fees
- High-yield savings with solid interest rates
- 24/7 customer service and easy-to-navigate app

Discover Bank
- No fees, plus cash back on debit card purchases
- Strong mobile experience and great for budgeting tools

Current
- Designed with younger users in mind
- Helpful saving/spending tools
- No fees and quick access to your paycheck with direct deposit

Opening your own bank account is one of the first real steps toward financial independence. You'll be able to manage your money, track your spending, and even set up direct deposits when you get a job or start a side hustle.

No more asking someone else to cash your checks.

This is your money, so make it official.

Wait! Where Did My Money Go? (a.k.a. Taxes 101)

So you finally got your first paycheck . . . but hold up! Why is the amount smaller than you expected? That's because of taxes. This is money taken out of your paycheck before it even hits your bank account. Here's what's going on:

Federal Taxes

This is money the US government takes to pay for big things like the military, national parks, education, and healthcare. Everyone pays federal taxes, no matter what state you live in.

State Taxes

If you live in a state that charges income tax (some don't!), your state takes a slice too. This helps pay for things like your local roads, public schools, and emergency services.

FICA Taxes (Social Security & Medicare)

This money supports two important programs:

- **Social Security:** Helps people after they retire.
- **Medicare:** Helps with medical costs when you're older. You're helping out your future self and today's seniors.

How to Estimate Your Take-Home Pay

Let's say your job offers $56,000 a year. Sounds nice, right?

But after taxes, you won't get the full $56,000 in your bank account. Use the site SmartAsset to get a realistic idea of your after-tax paycheck: www.smartasset.com/taxes/income-taxes. It even lets you pick your state so you can see exactly how much you'll really take home!

Then divide it by 12 to find your monthly take-home pay. This will help you budget more accurately.

Your Emergency Fund: The Ultimate Backup Plan

Life throws curveballs like flat tires, surprise medical bills, lost jobs, or laptops that decide to stop working right before finals. Having an **emergency fund** means you can handle unexpected hits without freaking out or swiping your credit card into debt.

Start small. Save a little from each paycheck, even if it's just $5 or $10. Over time, it adds up.

Once you've hit your starter goal, aim bigger. Most experts recommend keeping 3–6 months' worth of expenses in savings. That means if your monthly expenses (food, rent, gas, etc.) are $1,000, you should eventually try to have $3,000 to $6,000 saved.

Why? Because that kind of cushion gives you time. Time to find a new job, fix your car, or breathe during a crisis without going broke.

Store this emergency fund in your **savings account** or, even better, a **high-yield savings account** so it's safe, earns **interest**, and can still be accessed quickly if life throws a financial punch.

> **Important:** This money is for *real* emergencies. Not last-minute concert tickets, late-night takeout, or shoes you "accidentally" found on sale. Treat it like it's locked in a glass case labeled "Break Only in Case of Disaster."

Let's take a quick reality check: In a 2025 survey by *US News*, more than half of Americans said they felt *financially unprepared* for emergencies. Many reported stress about money, not having enough saved, or struggling to cover surprise expenses.[2]

It's no surprise, especially after what we saw during the 2020 pandemic. People lost jobs, hours were cut, bills kept coming, and suddenly that "rainy day" everyone talks about turned into a full-blown storm.

Life is unpredictable.

That's why your **emergency fund** is so important. It's your personal financial shield; it's a buffer between you and chaos. It

2. Erika Giovanetti, "Survey: 42% of Americans don't have an emergency fund," *US News*, January 22, 2025, https://www.usnews.com/banking/articles/2025-financial-wellness-survey.

helps you handle life's curveballs without panicking, taking on credit card debt, or draining every dollar you've got.

The good news? You don't have to save it all at once. Start small. Build over time.

Because peace of mind during hard times? That's priceless.

LEVEL UP

Your money is about to hit your account. Now it's time to take control of it like a boss.

Pick one thing you can do this week to level up your money game:

- ☐ Research and choose a no-fee banking app
- ☐ Open a checking or savings account
- ☐ Download your bank's mobile app and set up alerts
- ☐ Ask a parent or guardian to help open a teen account
- ☐ Compare banking options (local bank vs. online vs. credit union)

This week, I will: _____

START YOUR EMERGENCY FUND

(Yes, Even $5 Counts)

My goal this week:

- ☐ Save $5
- ☐ Save $10
- ☐ Move money into savings
- ☐ Research high-yield savings accounts

Why? Because peace of mind is priceless, and emergencies *will* happen.

MARY CONLAN

Back when my daughter was in high school, I wanted her to learn how to manage money early. Like a lot of teens, she was always asking for cash to hang out with friends or grab food. I didn't love the idea of her carrying around cash, and I wanted her to build some real-world financial skills, so we set her up with a debit card. It was under her name but was still connected to my account.

For the most part, it worked great. She learned how to check her balance, spend within her budget, and track where her money was going. She felt more independent, and I felt like I was helping her grow.

Until one day, everything changed.

She was about 18 when someone reached out to her online with what sounded like an amazing opportunity: deposit a $30,000 check, keep $5,000 for herself, and send the rest back to them. Easy money, right?

Wrong.

The check was fake. And because she deposited it into her account, the bank thought *she* was responsible. Within days, her account was massively overdrawn, and I started getting alerts. When I asked her what was going on, she froze. Embarrassed. Scared. Eventually, she broke down and told me everything.

We went straight to the police. She cried the whole way. The officer explained that even though she didn't mean to do anything wrong, the scam was serious, and if she didn't pay the full amount back, she could actually be charged with a crime.

She's still paying it off today—thousands of dollars she'll be working to repay for years. And since our accounts were connected, the bank took money from my savings and even from her siblings' accounts to try and cover it.

We thought a debit card would teach her responsibility, and in some ways, it did. But it also showed us how quickly things can go wrong when you don't fully understand how money, banks, and scams really work.

Just because something feels easy or sounds good doesn't mean it is. Being financially smart isn't just about earning and spending, it's about protecting what you've got. Scams are real, and they don't care how old or nice or smart you are. They just want your money.

So take this seriously. Ask questions. Learn how your bank account works. And if something feels off, don't do it.

That one decision cost our family more than $30,000. A mistake like that doesn't just go away.

A WORD FROM
LINDSEY BAKER

Some safety habits are just built in. I never forget to buckle my seatbelt, and I'm always on alert walking through a dark parking lot. But when it comes to money and digital safety, I'll admit that sometimes I let my guard down.

I was traveling through Guatemala. I did my research, found the safest ATMs, asked around, and played it smart. I was careful—like "triple check my wallet" careful. But one stop at an ATM was all it took, and someone cloned my debit card.

I didn't realize it at first. But then money started vanishing $300 at a time. Not all at once—just quietly, in sneaky little chunks like someone was testing how long they could get away with it.

Luckily, I caught it. But not because my bank texted me or raised a red flag. I caught it because I check my account often. It's just a habit now. And that habit saved me from losing even more. These days, you can set up automatic notifications to let you know any time money leaves your account. I strongly recommend it!

Financial safety isn't just about being careful; it's about being aware.

9

Budget Like a Boss

When you hear the word *budget*, what comes to mind? Boring spreadsheets? Grown-ups stressing over bills? Broke college students eating dry ramen?

We get it. Budgeting has a reputation, and it's not exactly cool. But here's the truth:

Budgeting isn't about restriction—it's about *freedom*.

Whether you're earning money from a part-time job, getting an allowance, running a side hustle, or babysitting on weekends, budgeting is your money map. It helps you hit your goals, avoid panic at checkout, and build confidence about your future.

Why You Actually Need a Budget (Yes, *You*)

Think budgeting is just for people drowning in debt or trying to survive adulthood? Think again.

Everyone—from millionaires to minimum-wage earners—needs to know where their money's going. If you don't tell your dollars what to do, they'll wander off and disappear.

Budgeting doesn't mean never buying an iced coffee or skipping fun. It means spending *on purpose*.

And that feeling when your savings actually grow? When you hit a goal you planned for? That's not boring. It's powerful.

Want to terrify yourself into taking control? Look at your last month of spending.

Add up:

- Fast food
- Subscriptions
- Random Amazon buys
- "It was only $5" moments

Now multiply it by 12.

Still think budgeting is boring?

So . . . What's a Budget, Really?

A **budget** is just a plan for your money.

That's it. It shows how much you make, what you spend it on, and what's left over. It helps you make choices that match your goals, not just your moods.

And the most important component for budgeting is savings.

If you check out the U.S. Bureau of Economic Analysis's updated monthly personal saving rate, it shows the percentage of disposable (after-tax) income that Americans are saving each month. Typically, it hovers around 4%. This number changes month to month, but it gives a real-time snapshot of how much the average person is putting away.[1]

Your ideal savings rate would be closer to 20%. That's not always achievable, especially when you're just starting out. But the closer you get, the more financial freedom and peace of mind you'll build for your future.

Budgeting Plans: Pick Your Money Map

Just like there's no "one right way" to decorate your room or organize your playlist, there's no one-size-fits-all budget. You can

---

1. See https://www.bea.gov/data/income-saving/personal-saving-rate.

build one that fits *your style* and goals. Here are two powerful but totally different ways to take control of your money.

Option 1: Zero-Based Budgeting (a.k.a. The "I Like Control" Method)

This one's for the planners. You assign every dollar a job until there's nothing left unaccounted for. Think of it like money Tetris. You win when every dollar fits perfectly into a category.

How It Works

1. **Figure out how much you made.**
   (From jobs, allowance, hustle, birthday cash—whatever hits your account.)
2. **Cover your needs.**
   Things like school lunches, gas, phone bill, or basics you're responsible for.
3. **Plan for fun money.**
   Yes, you *can* spend on movies, snacks, fashion, or Fortnite skins—just plan it first.
4. **See what's left over.**
   What's not already spent? This is the money you can put toward goals.
5. **Assign every dollar a purpose.**
   Saving for a car? College? A trip? Put that leftover money to work.

When you're done, your income – spending = $0.
That doesn't mean you're broke.
It means you *planned everything.*

Best for: Goal-getters, people who like tracking details, or anyone serious about saving.

Option 2: The 50/30/20 Plan
(a.k.a. The "Chill but Smart" Method)

This one's for the folks who want structure but don't want to track every $3 iced coffee.

Just split your money into 3 categories.

How It Works

1. **Figure out your total income.**
2. **Check how you've been spending.**
   Pull up your bank app or Venmo history. You might be shocked.
3. **Divide your monthly income into categories** and decide how much you can spend in each one. *See chart:*

Category	%	Examples
Needs	50%	groceries, gas, rent, phone bill, basic clothes, car payment
Wants	30%	games, subscriptions, takeout, concerts
Saving/Giving	20%	emergency fund, college savings, gifts, investments

4. **Adjust each month.** Life changes, so your budget should too.

Best for: Beginner budgeters, chill personalities, and people who like simplicity.

Budgeting doesn't have to be complicated, but it *does* have to be consistent. That's where the right tools come in.

Whether you're a tech-savvy app user or someone who prefers old-school systems, the goal is simple:

Find a money system that works for *you*, and actually use it.

Budgeting Apps:
Easy, and Gen Alpha/Z-Approved

Truth? You're probably on your phone a lot. So why not keep your budget there too?

These apps make it way easier to track your spending and see where your money's actually going. But heads up: some of them charge monthly fees or offer premium features that cost extra. Always read the fine print before signing up!

Here are a few budgeting apps worth checking out:

- **YNAB (You Need A Budget)**—Great for serious budgeters, but comes with a monthly fee after a free trial.
- **Rocket Money** (formerly Truebill)—Helps track subscriptions and spending, with optional upgrades.
- **PocketGuard**—Simple and user-friendly. Has a free version!
- **Goodbudget**—Based on the envelope system. Free plan includes up to 20 digital "envelopes."
- **NerdWallet**—Budgeting plus credit score tracking in one place.
- **Acorns**—Rounds up your purchases and invests the spare change. Small monthly fee applies.
- **Digit**—Helps you save automatically, but there's a fee after the free trial.
- **Rakuten**—Totally free. Earn cash back when you shop at major stores online.[2]
- **Empower**—Free financial planning and spending tracking tools (yep, free!).[3]

---

2. Jasmin Suknanan, "4 Apps to Help College Students Get their Finances Off to a Strong Start," CNBC, January 1, 2025, https://www.cnbc.com/select/money-apps-for-college-students/.

3. Taylor Tepper, "Best Budgeting Apps of 2025," Forbes, May 5, 2025, https://www.forbes.com/advisor/banking/best-budgeting-apps/.

Pro Tip: Start with a free version. Test it out for a month before committing to any paid features.

Envelope Budgeting: Old School (But It Works)

Not into apps? Try this: Cash in envelopes. For real.
Here's how it works:

- Label envelopes with spending categories
  (like gas, snacks, takeout, groceries, gifts).
- Put a set amount of cash in each.
- When it's gone—it's gone.

If you tend to swipe your debit card without thinking or tap Apple Pay like it's magic, this system makes you slow down and stay aware.

Pro Tip: You don't have to use envelopes for everything, just the areas where you overspend the most (hello, food and fashion).

And yes, you can totally DIY these envelopes with markers and sticky notes or grab some cool designs on Etsy or Amazon.

Apps for Splitting with Friends

Whether you're splitting pizza, gas, or concert tickets, things can get messy fast without a way to keep track.

These apps help keep it fair and keep the drama out of your friend group:

- **Venmo / Cash App / PayPal**—Quick and easy for paying each other back
- **Splitwise**—Tracks shared expenses over time (like rent) and tells you exactly who owes what
- **Splittr**—Perfect for group trips or recurring events (like school projects or party planning)

Using a split app might not sound "deep," but it can save a friendship. Money gets awkward fast, and these apps make it painless and fair.

Final Thought: Use What You'll Stick With

The best budgeting tool isn't the one with the most features or fancy charts. It's the one you'll actually use.

- If you like tracking things digitally → try an app
- If you need physical reminders → try cash envelopes
- If you're managing group money → use a split app
- If you want total control → try zero-based budgeting

Your budget = your system.

Find your rhythm, tweak it as needed, and keep going.

You don't need to wait until you're 25 and stressed to get smart about money.

Start now. Start small. Just start.

And remember: The best budget isn't the most complicated one. It's the one you'll actually use.

You're the boss of your money. Budget like it.

LEVEL UP

Your money = your choices. Let's build a system that actually works for *you*.

Before you make a plan, you've got to see the truth. Pull up your banking app, cash app, or Venmo history from the last 30 days and take a close look.

Choose Your Budget Style:

- ☐ **Zero-Based Budgeting—I want full control over every dollar**
- ☐ **50/30/20 Plan—I want a simple structure I can stick to**
- ☐ **Cash Envelope System—I need a physical system to stay on track**
- ☐ **Budgeting App—I want to track everything on my phone**

This week, I'll test: _____

SET YOUR BUDGET GOALS

What I'm saving for: _____

Amount I want to save:$_____

Target date: _____

Now ask yourself:

What can I cut or reduce to reach that faster?

_____

A WORD FROM

BLAKE TORRES

Back when I was in grad school, life was pretty simple and pretty broke. My wife and I were living in a tiny two-bedroom, one-bath house, making it work on my student loans and her teacher salary. In other words, money was TIGHT.

One morning, I was getting ready to head out early for a big exam. My wife had already left for work, and I was hustling to get out the door. But when I got to my car—bad news: the gas gauge was sitting on E (empty).

No big deal, I thought. *I can probably coast to the gas station . . .*

Just to be safe, I checked our bank account.

Negative balance.

Checked the credit card.

Maxed out.

Awesome.

To make it worse, my wife's paycheck wasn't coming in until the *next day*.

I ran back inside, tearing through drawers and couch cushions, hunting for coins like it was a treasure hunt.

Nothing.

Not even a dusty penny.

I sat there thinking, *Now what?*

Then, light bulb moment.

I remembered that $3 charge I always saw on my phone bill—AT&T Roadside Assistance. Included with it? Three free gallons of gas, delivered wherever you are.

I called them up, and sure enough, a truck showed up at our house and filled my tank with just enough gas to get me through the day. (Shout out to Past Me for signing up for that $3 plan without even knowing how clutch it would be.)

I honestly don't even remember if I crushed that exam or not, but you better believe that after that day, we started hiding a $20 bill in every car we owned . . . just in case we ever got stuck like that again.

A WORD FROM

ALICIA BENNETT

I work at a high school, where I help students navigate their futures, cheer them on at pep rallies, and write glowing rec letters. You'd think I'd have this "adulting" thing down. But let me tell you about the year I learned a hard financial lesson.

It started with a form. You know those W-4 forms HR hands you when you start a job? I filled it out just like I was supposed to. I even double-checked the boxes. I handed it over and didn't think twice.

For months, everything seemed normal. My paychecks came in, I built my budget, I paid my bills. I wasn't out here living like a Kardashian, but I felt pretty responsible.

Then tax season hit.

I was expecting a small refund, maybe enough for a nice dinner or to throw into savings. But instead, my jaw hit the floor.

I *owed* thousands.

Turns out, HR made a mistake when processing my form. They didn't withhold the federal taxes from my checks. So while I was budgeting with what looked like a regular paycheck, I was really being paid like an independent contractor with no taxes taken out.

Now I'm working summer school during the day and picking up a second shift at a restaurant at night just to pay off what I owe. I'm exhausted. And mad. But mostly? I'm a little wiser.

Always check your pay stub. I know it sounds boring. But understanding what's being withheld, and what isn't, can save you from a big mess later.

Trust me, it's a lot better to catch a mistake early than to be hit with a surprise bill from Uncle Sam while you're just trying to live your life.

10

Let's Talk Debt

Have you ever heard someone say:

- ✗ "You'll always have debt."
- ✗ "That's just life."
- ✗ "You can't go to college without student loans."

Let's hit pause on that.

Yeah, debt might be *common*, but that doesn't mean it's beneficial. Saying "everyone has debt" is like saying "everyone gets sunburned" and then never using sunscreen.

So what *is* debt, really?

Debt is when you owe money to someone else. Sounds simple, right? But here's the catch: When you're in debt, your future paycheck is already spoken for. You're working for someone else before you even get paid. And that's not freedom, that's financial handcuffs.

These days, you can borrow money for *anything*, including college, phones, cars, Amazon purchases, furniture, concerts, clothes, and even food delivery, with just a tap. That's called **financing**: when you borrow money now and agree to pay it back later.

Plot twist: You pay back more than you borrow. Like . . . *a lot* more.

Interest is a powerful force in personal finance. It can either work *for you* or work *against you*.

At its core, interest is what you *earn* when you let others use your money and what you *pay* when you borrow money from someone else (like a bank or credit card company).

Interest works against you when you finance items. This happens when you borrow money with buy now/pay later apps.

Let's say you're moving into your first apartment and want that $1,200 couch from the furniture store. They offer a "buy now, pay later" deal: just $100 a month for 15 months. Sounds chill, right?

Nope. After interest and sneaky fees, you end up paying *over $1,600* for a couch (depreciable item) that's already seen every season of *The Office* twice.

And the worst part? You probably could've snagged the same couch (or at least a close cousin) on Facebook Marketplace for like $100 and a slice of pizza.

Financing is designed to stretch out payments to make them more "manageable," but it quietly blows up the price tag.

So, Is *Any* Debt Okay?

You might've heard:

- ✕ "Student loans are good debt."
- ✕ "Mortgages are good debt."

Truth?

There's no such thing as "good debt" if it leaves you stressed, broke, or stuck.

Sure, some debt might be *worth it,* like a student loan for a degree that leads to a higher paying career or a loan with a low interest rate for an appreciating asset, like a house. But even then, the key is to:

- → Borrow the least amount possible.
- → Know what you're getting into.

→ And understand the true total cost, not just the
monthly payment.

The Types of Debt You Might See After High School

Student Loans!

This is the most common first debt teens take on. If used wisely,
it's an investment. If ignored or mismanaged, it can become a
financial nightmare. (*See Chapter 14.*)

Tech & Phone Payment Plans

That shiny iPhone 16? $30/month sounds chill . . . until you miss
a payment. Miss enough and your phone gets shut off and your
credit score tanks.

Tip: Save first, buy later.

Credit Cards

You can't legally get one alone until you're 18, but companies
start marketing them early, and sometimes parents co-sign "to
help build credit." (*See chapter 11.*)

Be careful. Credit cards have the highest interest rates and
are designed to keep you paying interest for years. Paying just the
minimum means your $200 purchase could cost $500+ over time.

Buy Now, Pay Later (BNPL)

Apps like Afterpay, Klarna, and Affirm are trending hard. You
buy sneakers today, pay them off over weeks. Sounds cool, right?

Until you forget a payment, get hit with late fees, and end up
spending more than if you'd just saved up first.

Picture this, you're at Coachella, dancing in the desert, posting fire selfies, and living your best life. But here's the not-so-
glamorous side: about 60% of festival-goers used Buy Now, Pay

Later to get their tickets.[1] That means for thousands of people, the music stopped but the payments kept going.

The tickets might be split into "easy" payments, but if you're still paying for a concert after the headliner has dropped a whole new album, that's not a good deal. It's a financial hangover.

The Ripple Effect of Debt

Debt doesn't just take money out of your wallet; it can delay almost everything you want in life.

Think of debt like throwing a heavy backpack on before a race. It weighs you down, slows your momentum, and makes every step harder.

Here's what that can look like:

- You want to move out?
    - That's tough if your loan payments eat half your paycheck. Rent, deposit, utilities all add up fast.

- Thinking about travel?
    - That dream trip might have to wait. When you're paying off debt, it's hard to save for anything extra.

- Want to start a business or take a risk?
    - Monthly payments mean less freedom to take chances. Debt makes you think smaller, not bigger.

- Trying to build credit?
    - Ironically, too much debt can hurt your credit score, making it harder to rent an apartment or get a decent car loan.

---

1. Jack Kelly, "The Buy Now, Pay Later Boom at Coachella, Signs of Stretched Wallets," *Forbes*, April 16, 2025, https://www.forbes.com/sites/jackkelly/2025/04/16/the-buy-now-pay-later-boom-at-coachella-signs-of -stretched-wallets/.

- Want to buy a house later?
  - Lenders look at your debt-to-income ratio. If you're already buried in payments, they may say no, even if your income is solid.

- Looking to start a family someday?
  - Children are amazing but expensive. Debt might delay decisions like marriage, homeownership, or kids, simply because your finances aren't ready.

The world is set up to make debt look normal, easy, and even smart. However, the less debt you carry, the more options you have. Simple as that.

Being debt free doesn't mean you're rich. It means your money is yours and not promised to a bank, app, or credit card company.

Start building smart habits now like saving before you spend, knowing what things *really* cost, borrowing only when absolutely necessary, and making it your mission to be debt free as early as possible.

LEVEL UP

Debt might feel normal, but freedom is better. Here's how to start owning your money before it owns you.

Choose one "debt trap" you want to avoid starting now:

- ☐ **Buy Now, Pay Later apps**
- ☐ **Credit cards until I'm financially ready**
- ☐ **Spending money I haven't earned yet**
- ☐ **Paying only the minimum on a credit card each month**
- ☐ **Borrowing without understanding interest or terms**

I commit to avoiding: _____

Now write one simple habit or move you can make this week to build financial freedom instead of debt.

This week, I will: _____

A WORD FROM

MATTHEW NELSON

Before I even graduated, I already had a mountain of debt hanging over me. And I *hated* it.

I'd actually been debt free once before, and I realized something big: Debt is like modern-day indentured servitude. That thought changed everything.

I went into full hustle-and-scramble mode:

- Cooked almost every meal at home
- Learned to do my own car repairs
- And drove a hand-me-down 1995 Nissan Altima with 340,000 miles on it. Yes, seriously. It had cold AC, heat that worked, and it sipped gas like a pro. My parents gave it to me with 240,000 miles and said, *"Just leave it on the side of the road if it blows up; we already got our money's worth."*

Since I was tired of being broke, I needed to flip the script and *earn more money.* So I started researching where I could get paid the most and fast.

Alaska stood out. Why?

- No state income tax
- No sales tax in many areas
- 25–40% higher pay than most other states (because not many people want to move there)

Sure, the cost of living was higher, but with *no taxes* and *bigger paychecks,* the math worked. When the job offer came through, I didn't hesitate.

Fast forward one year later . . .

I've been living and working in one of the most beautiful places on Earth for over a year now. I've paid off $59,000 in debt, which is almost 30% of the total I started with. And at this pace, I'm on track to be 100% debt free in just a few more years. About 85% of my spending goes toward debt, rent, bills, and food. The rest? I save, travel, and invest in my freedom.

The Alaska plan is working.

Takeaways:

→ Debt is heavy. Avoid it if you can. If you can't: attack it head-on.
→ Live below your means. It's not forever, but it gives you power.
→ Be creative. Sometimes the best opportunity is where no one else wants to go.
→ Money = options. And the earlier you start building smart habits, the sooner you get those options.

11

Credit: Swipe Now, Regret Later?

Don't you just love that beautiful plastic magic? That shiny little rectangle you can tap on a machine like a wizard casting a spell—*ding!*

It's fast. It's easy. Cash seems archaic, but credit is in style.

Using a credit card feels like pulling out a wand and saying, "Accio new shoes!" and the universe just delivers. No pain. No sacrifice. Just a swipe and some good vibes.

It's a financial trust fall with a bank.

They whisper, "Go ahead. We got you."

But what they don't say out loud is: " . . . and we'll be charging you for the fall. With interest."

Credit cards let you borrow money that isn't yours, and if you don't pay it back quickly, it's like the price tag grows teeth.

Imagine you finally snag that $90 pro gaming mouse: the one with RGB lights, 12 buttons, and click speed that could win tournaments. You just have to swipe your credit card.

But if you miss a payment or only pay the minimum, and suddenly that mouse is costing you way more. With interest and fees? You could end up paying $130, maybe $150, for something that was supposed to level up your game, not your debt.

You might be thinking: *Isn't this just like a debit card? What's the big deal?*

Let's clear that up:

Credit Card = Borrowed Magic

You're spending their money. It's like renting your stuff . . . with interest.

Debit Card = Real Money

You're spending your own cash from your bank account. If it's not there, it won't let you spend it. It keeps you grounded.

Credit is a tool, like a chainsaw.
Use it right? You can build something amazing.
Use it wrong? You could cut off your financial future.

And here's the great part: most teens don't even have credit yet, which means you're likely learning about this before the game starts.

Let's make sure you don't walk into the game without a game plan.

Real-Life Stuff Credit Affects

1. **Your First Car Loan**—Bad credit = higher monthly payments.
2. **College Life**—Cosigners, student loan rates, and even student housing can be affected by your credit.
3. **Phone Plans**—Yep, some companies check your credit before giving you a contract.
4. **Your First Apartment**—Landlords look at your credit to see if you'll pay on time.
5. **Your Future Job**—Some employers check credit, especially for jobs handling money or data.

So, What's a Credit Score?

Think of your **credit score** like a reputation meter for your money habits. The higher the number, the more trustworthy you look to banks and businesses.

Here's the score breakdown[1]:

Score	Rating	Meaning
800–850	Excellent	You're a financial rockstar
740–799	Very Good	You're doing great
670–739	Good	Keep it up
580–669	Fair	Some red flags here
Below 580	Poor	Time to rebuild trust

Credit in Action: The Expensive Car Mistake

Let's say someone buys a car for $41,138. Seems like a big purchase, but not wild, right? But the person purchasing the car is in the fair credit range.

Now check this out[2]:

- **Interest rate:** 13% (fair credit = higher interest)
- **Interest Total:** $18,334 *whoa*
- **Total cost after 6 years:** $59,472
- **Monthly payment:** $826

Think of what that $18,000 difference could have bought instead.

1. Amanda Barroso, "Credit Score Ranges: Where You Fall and How to Improve Your Standing," NerdWallet, April 3, 2025, https://www.nerdwallet.com/article/finance/credit-score-ranges-and-how-to-improve.
2. Shannon Bradley, "Average Car Loan Interest Rates by Credit Score," NerdWallet, May 5, 2025, https://www.nerdwallet.com/article/loans/auto-loans/average-car-loan-interest-rates-by-credit-score.

How to Build Credit *Without* Getting into Debt

You don't need to be rich or rack up debt to build good credit. Here's your Credit Starter Pack:

1. Always pay on time.

Even one missed payment can seriously hurt your score.

2. Use a credit card wisely.

Charge small things (like gas or food), then pay it off *in full* every month. Only paying the minimum on a credit card keeps you in debt longer, racks up interest, and turns small purchases into expensive long-term burdens.

3. Don't max out your card.

Use less than 30% of your credit limit.[3] If you max out your card or get too close to the limit, it can hurt your credit score even if you always make your payments. Keeping it low tells lenders you know how to manage money well.

4. Check your credit reports.

Look for errors or fraud. Get your free credit reports at sites like **AnnualCreditReport.com**.

Think of your credit score like XP in a video game. You level up by making smart money moves by paying on time, keeping balances low, and using credit wisely. But ghost your payments or max out your cards and you'll lose progress fast.

Credit is not your enemy, and it is not free money. It is a tool. Use it right and it can unlock doors: apartments, jobs, even lower interest rates. Use it wrong and it can hold you back.

So play smart. Build wisely.

---

3. Lauren Schwahn, "How Much of My Credit Card Should I Use?" NerdWallet, February 15, 2024, https://www.nerdwallet.com/article/finance/30-percent-ideal-credit-utilization-ratio-rule.

LEVEL UP

Let's make sure that you are in control of your money, not the banks. Grab your journal and write the following.

One future thing I want good credit for: _____

You might not have credit *yet*, but it's coming. Here's your move . . .

Pick one healthy credit habit you'll start with:

- ☐ **Pay bills (like phone or subscriptions) on time**
- ☐ **Learn how to check your credit report**
- ☐ **Set up autopay for any recurring payments**
- ☐ **Only use a credit card if I can pay it off in full**
- ☐ **Keep credit usage under 30% of the limit**

A WORD FROM

KATHERINE MATSON

We grew up poor. And in a small town where everyone knows your business, that carries a lot of shame. We were always acutely aware of our limits, what we could and couldn't afford to buy or do. My father had a firm rule: he only bought what he could afford at the time, which often wasn't much. But beyond that general awareness, we never really talked about money. There were no meaningful discussions about fiscal responsibility.

When I turned 18 and got my first credit card, I felt a financial freedom I'd never known before. I wasn't limited to what my meager hostessing job could afford. I could buy what I wanted right now. It was glorious . . . until that first bill came due. My job barely paid enough to cover gas, let alone a credit card bill. And when you're young with no credit, you don't exactly get a high limit, so maxing out a card happens fast. I had no idea how credit worked, how deeply it affected your ability to rent an apartment, buy a car, qualify for loans, or even get certain jobs. By the time I learned, I was in my mid-20s and my credit was in the gutter. I had multiple maxed-out cards, had unpaid bills in collections, and was once again living paycheck to paycheck.

One day on the way to work, the $3,000 car I'd bought in cash finally died. How it lasted as long as it did is still a feat of modern mechanics. I needed something reliable and fast. But I didn't have money saved, and my credit was too poor to get a loan. I had to ask my dad to co-sign. As a grown adult who should have had her life together, it was humiliating. There it was again, the shame I'd grown up with. Not being able to do the basic things others seemed to find so easy. It's hard to build a life when you're just trying to survive.

That was the moment everything changed. I had a job that allowed me to cover my rent, my car payment, and go out with friends once in a while. But I knew if something unexpected happened (car trouble, a medical bill, etc.), I'd be screwed. I was tired of feeling like a victim of my circumstances. So I pulled my credit report and got to work.

I started with the collections. I called and negotiated payoffs or set up payment plans. I made sure "paid in full" letters were sent to the credit bureaus. Then I made a budget to pay down my credit cards. I relearned an old lesson from childhood: if I couldn't afford to buy it outright, I didn't buy it. Only spending what was in my checking account helped me avoid impulsive purchases. As the debt shrank, I spent less on interest and finally began putting money into savings.

When I turned 30, I decided I needed a fresh start. I drained most of my savings to rent a U-Haul, drove across the country, and started over. It felt terrifying, but it was the best decision I could've made. In a new city with no history and no baggage, I was free to let go of the "poor kid" narrative I'd never been able to outrun. I had spent five years in the real estate industry not really taking my career seriously. Now, I gave it everything. I advanced, got promoted, and stayed strategic with my finances. I opened a 401(k), built up $50,000 in savings, and raised my credit score from the low 600s to 790.

A big part of my progress came from learning how to live intentionally below my means. Even as my income grew, I didn't let my spending grow with it. I stopped chasing the quick dopamine hit of buying myself things and focused instead on the long-term reward of financial stability. And that stability hasn't just brought peace of mind—it's given me the freedom to prioritize what truly matters. I've been able to travel more, invest in my passion for photography, and spend money on experiences I can share with the people I love: weekend trips with friends, concerts, plays, or just a great dinner out. These are the things that make me feel rich in the ways that count.

Even if you grow up completely financially illiterate, you *can* teach yourself how to do better. It's not easy, especially when you're starting from behind, but the effort is worth it. Financial literacy is a slow climb, and shame can make it feel even steeper. But the moment you decide to stop surviving and start building, you begin to change the trajectory of your life.

12

Cool Car,
Empty Wallet?

Not gonna lie. Getting your first car is exciting. It's freedom. It's independence. It's "blasting music with your friends on the way to Taco Bell at 10 p.m." good.

But your first car is also one of the biggest financial decisions you'll make as a young adult. And if you're not careful, it can wreck your wallet before you even start your career.

Spoiler: Your car doesn't define who you are. But it might define how broke or how free you feel five years from now.

You've seen it online: luxury cars, tricked-out trucks, dream Jeeps. It's easy to feel like your car needs to be a flex.

But guess what?

Your car's job is to get you from point A to point B, not to impress people at stoplights.

Chasing status on four wheels might look cool now . . .

But $400/month car payments hit *very differently* when you're also trying to save to pay college loans, move out, or buy your first place.

Which Ride Sets You Up Best?

A realistic look at car choices, monthly payments, and long-term impact.

Car Option	Est. Monthly Payment	Total Cost Over 5 Years	What You're Paying For	Monthly Savings vs. 4Runner	If You Invested That Difference for 20 Years (8% Return)[a]
New 4Runner	~$900	~$54,000+	Brand-new, flashy, off-road capable, high insurance & gas	$0	$0 (you're maxed out)
New Toyota Camry	~$400	~$24,000	Safe, fuel-efficient, great features	~$500/month	~$285,000
Used 5-Year-Old Camry	~$250	~$15,000	Reliable, lower cost on everything	~$650/month	~$370,000

[a] See https://www.calculator.net/investment-calculator

The bottom line is that you don't have to live like a monk. But just know that every big purchase comes with a hidden cost: what that money could've done for you over time.

One smart car choice today could be the reason future-you is sitting on a beach, laptop closed, without a single car payment in sight.

Top 5 First Car Tips (From People Who've Been There)

1. Buy used—reliable beats shiny.
You can find clean, dependable cars under $10k if you take your time. Check sites like Edmunds, KBB, Carfax, or even local sellers.

2. Don't "monthly payment" yourself into debt.
Car dealers love asking, "What monthly payment are you looking for?" That question is a trap. Focus on the total cost, not just the payment.

3. Fixing an old car is often cheaper than buying new.
A $1,500 repair might sound scary, until you compare it to $20,000 in new car debt. Always do the math.

4. Know what you actually need.
Do you *need* a truck, or do you just like how it looks? Be honest about your lifestyle, your budget, and what fits both.

5. Set a limit and stick. to. it.
Before you step foot on a lot or open a car listing, decide your max budget. Write it down. Stick to it. No matter how cool the rims are.

Car Buying Prep Checklist

- ☐ I know my true needs (not just my wants).
- ☐ I've checked used listings and prices.
- ☐ I've looked up car values on KBB or Edmunds.
- ☐ I've figured out how much I can spend *without a loan*.
- ☐ I'm ready to walk away if it doesn't feel right.

The goal isn't to have the coolest car in the school lot.

The goal is to still have money left over for the *next* lot—your apartment, your job, your dream trip.

Your first car should get you where you want to go in life, not just on the road.

LEVEL UP

Your first car shouldn't be the thing that drives your wallet into a ditch. Let's map out a better route.

In your journal, list your dream car then write down what you *actually need* in a car right now.

Dream Car: _____

What I actually need: Check all the boxes you want your first car decision to pass:

- ☐ **Under $10k (or close to it)**
- ☐ **Fuel efficient**
- ☐ **Safe and reliable**
- ☐ **Doesn't require a loan**
- ☐ **Leaves room to still save or invest**
- ☐ **Makes me feel responsible, not just impressed**

THE LONG-TERM LENS

What could you do with an extra $_____ /month if you *didn't* have a huge car payment?

This week, I will:

- ☐ Research 3 used cars in my budget
- ☐ Talk to someone who's made a smart (or not-so-smart) car decision
- ☐ Make a car-buying budget and commit to it

A WORD FROM
JOE ROACH

Back when I was a baby pharmacist, fresh out of school with a shiny name tag and a mountain of student loans, I thought I was living the dream. I had a steady paycheck, a professional title, and not one but two car payments.

But I was not living the dream. Between loan payments, rent, and those two metal boxes with wheels draining my bank account, I was barely living at all.

Eventually, I had a wake-up call. I was tired of feeling like I worked full time just to make payments on things I already regretted buying. So I made a decision: no more consumer debt. I hustled, budgeted, skipped the lattes (okay, not all of them), and slowly climbed my way out.

Years later, debt free and proud, I walked into a dealership ready to buy a new (to me) car. The salesman greeted me with the usual line: "What monthly payment are you looking for?"

I smiled. "Just one."

He blinked. "Wait, you mean . . . you're not financing?"

"Nope," I said. "I'm paying cash."

His face froze like I just told him I moonlight as a superhero. "Is that even possible?"

It is. And I've never had a car payment since.

Moral of the story? Debt doesn't have to be your default. The real flex isn't the fancy car—it's owning it outright.

13

Investing: How to Grow Your Dough

Wait. Why should you even care about investing?

Look, we get it. "Investing" sounds like something your uncle Gary does while watching cable news and shouting at the TV. But the thing is, if you start learning how to invest now, you get something most adults would literally fight a raccoon to have: **time**.

The earlier you start, the more money your money makes. It's called **compound interest**. Basically, your money earns money, and then that money earns money. It's the financial version of cloning your dollar bills and making them work overtime.

Let's break it down: simple, smart, and maybe even a little fun.

The 3 Basic Types of Investments (a.k.a. Choose Your Fighter)

Investment Type	What It Means	Risk Level	Long-Term Average Return
Cash Equivalents	Fancy term for savings accounts & **CDs** (certificate of deposit)	Low	1–3%
Bonds	You loan money and get interest	Medium	4–6%
Stocks	You own part of a company—fancy!	High	8–11%

Higher risk = higher reward. But chill. Playing the long game helps balance it out.

Mutual Funds & ETFs: The Snack Packs of Investing

Instead of betting on just one company, mutual funds and ETFs let you invest in a whole bundle of companies at once. It's like buying a bag of trail mix instead of only cashews.

→ **Mutual Funds** = Managed by humans. Bought/sold at the end of the day. May have higher minimum investments. Often used in retirement accounts or older styles of investing.

→ **ETFs (Exchange Traded Funds)** = Usually follow the market. You can buy/sell it during the day, like a stock. Often has super low fees. Good for beginners who want flexibility. You'll need a brokerage account (like Fidelity, Schwab, etc.)

What Is an Index?

A stock market index is a list or group of companies used to measure how a part of the market is doing. It is like a scoreboard for the stock market.

Famous Examples

Index	What It Tracks
S&P 500	500 of the biggest US companies
Dow Jones	30 major US companies
Nasdaq 100	100 large tech-heavy companies

Best Beginner Move?
Go for Index Fund ETFs with Low Fees.

Why? Less Drama. More Growth.

Let's break it down.

An index fund isn't its own type of investment; it's more like a strategy that can be *packaged* in different ways.

That strategy = Instead of trying to beat the market, I'll just be the market.

You're probably not trying to be the next wolf on Wall Street. You just want your money to grow while you focus on school, your hobbies, and maybe your side hustle. That's where **index funds** come in.

Imagine an index fund like a giant smoothie. Each fruit in the smoothie is a different company: like Apple, Nike, or Netflix. Instead of buying just one company's stock (like only strawberries), an index fund lets you sip on a blend of hundreds of top companies all at once.

This gives you:

→ **Instant diversification**
   (a.k.a. "don't put all your eggs in one basket")
→ **Lower risk**
   (because if one company tanks, others can balance it out)
→ **Peace of mind**
   (no need to constantly check the stock market)

One of the best-known index funds follows the S&P 500, which includes 500 of the biggest companies in America. If the overall market grows (and historically, it always has over time), your money grows too. Less stress. Lower fees. Proven results over decades.

Investing in an index fund is one of the smartest moves you can make for your future.

And if you don't trust me, take it from the GOAT investor, Warren Buffet: *"By periodically investing in an index fund, the know-nothing investors can actually outperform most investment professionals."*

Where Can You Get an Index Fund?

You're not walking into a store with a shopping cart for this one. Buying an index fund is all digital, and it's easier than you think. Here's where teens (and anyone) can start:

- **#1 Choice: Robinhood**—Popular app with a simple interface, commission-free trades, and easy access to index funds.
- **Fidelity**—Offers a Youth Account for teens ages 13–17 (with a parent). Super beginner-friendly.
- **Charles Schwab**—Great platform for first-time investors, with no account minimums.
- **Vanguard**—The OG of index funds (they *literally* created the first one). Long-term investing vibes.
- **Public, M1 Finance, or SoFi**—Easy-to-use investing apps with cool designs and no required minimum to get started.

> **Heads up:** If you're under 18, you'll need a custodial account, which means a parent or guardian signs up with you. But YOU still get to learn, watch your money grow, and make decisions together.

Starter Index Funds to Look Up

- ☐ **VOO** (S&P 500—tracks the top 500 US companies)
- ☐ **VTI** (Total US Stock Market—from Vanguard)
- ☐ **FXAIX** (Fidelity's S&P 500 fund—super low fees)

Your Money + Time = FIRE

Let's say you invest only $1,000 in an index fund at age 18 with an average annual return of 8%:

- At 18 = $1,000
- At 28 = $2,159
- At 38 = $4,660
- At 48 = $10,062
- At 58 = $21,725

Add more regularly? Now you're really cooking with compounded returns.

Top 3 Investing Myths—DEBUNKED

1. **"Investing is only for rich people."**
   - × Nah. You can start with less than the price of a pizza.

2. **"You have to be a genius to invest."**
   - × If you can understand TikTok trends, you can understand investing.

3. **"It's too risky."**
   - × So is buying $12 boba tea every day. Start small. Learn as you go.

Stocks: Owning a Piece of the Action

Imagine walking into an Apple store and saying, "Hi, I'm one of the owners. Just browsing."

You wouldn't be lying.

When you buy stock in a company, you own a tiny piece of that business.

Own 100 shares of Apple (ticker symbol: AAPL)? You're officially part-owner of Apple—congrats! That means you've got real voting rights and a theoretical seat at shareholder meetings (okay, maybe way in the back behind a bunch of guys in suits).

A **share** is a tiny piece of ownership in a company. The **price of a share** is how much it costs to buy one of those pieces. So if a share of a company costs $10, and you buy two shares, you own a $20 slice of that company.

Owning stock = owning a slice of the action.

How You Make Money from Stocks

There are two major ways stocks put cash in your pocket:

1. Stock Price Going Up (Stock Appreciation)

When a company does well, people want to own part of it. More buyers = higher prices.

If you buy stock at $20 and later sell it at $40—congratulations, you just doubled your money. Be careful because if you buy and sell stock quickly, then you have higher taxes on your gains. But if you hold your investments for more than a year, the IRS gives you a break with lower tax rates.

2. Dividends (Cash Rewards)

Some companies share a slice of their profits with stockholders.

These are called **dividends**. Think of them as thank-you payments just for being an owner.

Companies like Starbucks (SBUX) and Coca-Cola (KO) send dividends every few months.

Not every company pays dividends though. Fast-growing ones like to reinvest their profits to grow bigger.

Why Owning Stocks Is a Big Deal

→ Highest potential long-term growth compared to other places you can put your money (like bonds or savings accounts).

→ Pride. It's cool to say you own part of the brands you love.

→ Excitement. Watching your investments grow can be addictive (in a good way).

But . . . There Are Risks Too

× Stocks are a rollercoaster. Prices go up and down. Some days you'll feel rich. Some days, not so much. (Just ask GameStop buyers)

× No backup plan if you only own one stock. If your one company tanks (hello, Blockbuster and Enron), your money could vanish with it.

× Companies can go bankrupt. Even giant companies have fallen apart fast when they made bad decisions.

Timing Matters

The Stock Market Always Comes Back
(If You're Patient)

The stock market has big swings. It crashes. It rallies. It's like a heartbeat—up, down, up, down.

But over the long term, the trend has always been UP.

• Through world wars
• Through recessions
• Through pandemics

That chart below? That's 50 years of the S&P 500. This comprises the top 500 companies in the U.S. economy. Lots of dips. Lots of drama. But the direction? Still up.

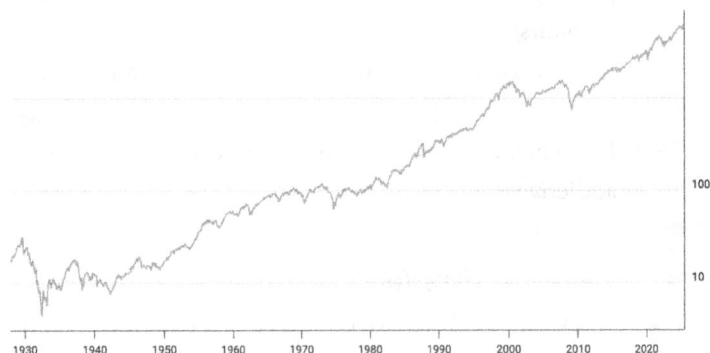

Figure 1: S&P 500 stock market index since 1927
Source: "S&P 500 Index - 100 Year Historical Chart." MacroTrends. Accessed July 6, 2025.
https://www.macrotrends.net/2324/sp-500-historical-chart-data.

In early 2020, when the COVID-19 pandemic swept across the globe, fear gripped the world, and the stock market took a steep dive, wiping out trillions of dollars in value. Headlines screamed panic, and many people, overwhelmed by uncertainty, rushed to sell their stocks, even if it meant selling with a loss. They were scared things would only get worse.

However, not too long after, the market recovered and kept climbing. In fact, it eventually reached all-time highs. What looked like a total collapse was actually just a massive, temporary dip. Those who stayed steady when things got shaky saw their investments bounce back stronger than ever.

In the stock market, it's not about timing every up and down. If you zoom out and look at the big picture, the US stock market has always grown in the long run.

Risky Business

Investing always comes with risk. That means there's a chance your money might go down before it goes up. Some people hear that and get nervous, but risk isn't something to be afraid of; it's just part of how investing works. In fact, without risk, there's no reward. The reason people earn money over time in the stock market is because they're willing to deal with some ups and downs along the way.

The good news is, you don't have to take wild risks to be a good investor. Smart investors use a strategy called **diversification** and a great way to understand that is by thinking about video games.

Imagine you're playing a game where you can collect different tools, weapons, or power-ups. You wouldn't go into a tough level with just one item, right? If that item fails, you're stuck. But if you have a mix of gear—maybe some defense, some speed, some attack power—you're more prepared for whatever the game throws at you. That's how diversification works with money. Instead of putting all your money into one stock or one company, you spread it out across different investments. That way, if one part drops in value, the others can help balance things out.

You won't always win right away. But diversification helps protect you and keeps you in the game for the long run. Managing risk isn't about avoiding challenges. It's about being ready for them. And just like in gaming, a good strategy beats luck almost every time.

When you start investing, start small. Think long term. Own companies you believe in. You don't need to be rich, famous, or wearing a three-piece suit to invest. You just need to start. Be consistent. Be curious. Be patient.

Let your money work for you while you're out living your life.

LEVEL UP

Taking the first steps in investing can be scary. Let's keep it simple.

DECODE YOUR INVESTOR TYPE

Which one sounds most like you?

- ☐ "I'm a total beginner. I just learned what an index fund is."
- ☐ "I want to start with apps and see what happens."
- ☐ "I want to invest, but I don't know where to begin."
- ☐ "I want long-term growth, not fast cash."

Why I want to invest (or learn to):

Pick *one* investing platform or app and check it out (Robinhood, Fidelity Youth, Vanguard, Charles Schwab, Public, etc.).

Look for:

- ☐ No or low fees
- ☐ Easy-to-use app or site
- ☐ Index funds or ETFs
- ☐ Educational tools

Platform I researched: _____

One thing I liked: _____

Even if you're not investing *today*, make a plan for what you'd like to do.

- ☐ Open a custodial or youth investing account
- ☐ Start with $10–$50 in an index fund
- ☐ Ask a parent or adult to help walk through an app together
- ☐ Watch 1–2 beginner videos on investing basics
- ☐ Build a "wishlist" of companies or funds you want to invest in

This week, I will: _____

A WORD FROM
MIKE RYBURN

Let me take you back to the mid-1980s.

I had just heard a hot tip from a friend: a bank called Worthen was doing well and its stock was selling for just $7.50 a share. I figured I'd throw in a little: 100 shares for $750 sounded reasonable. So I picked up the phone—because back then, you actually had to call a real person to buy stocks. No apps, no slick dashboards, no tap-to-invest buttons.

Today, you can open a brokerage app on your phone in five minutes, scroll through hundreds of stocks, and buy with the same ease you order fries. You see a price, tap once or twice, and boom—you're an investor.

Back then? One slightly fuzzy phone call and you were in for a wild financial ride.

I called my broker and said, "I'd like to buy a hundred shares of Worthen, please."

He heard: "Eight hundred shares."

I didn't know it yet, but I had just accidentally invested $6,000 instead of $750. That's like ordering a pizza and getting charged for the whole restaurant's tab.

A few days later, I opened my mailbox, saw the trade confirmation, and nearly passed out. I had eight times the shares I meant to buy. Total panic hit.

I sprinted to the newspaper (our ancient version of checking stock prices) and saw that Worthen had already gone up a bit to almost $8 a share. I took a deep breath and thought: "Well . . . I guess I'm in this now."

And I held on. For years.

Here's what happened:

Worthen was bought out by another bank, which then got bought by NationsBank, which eventually merged with (you guessed it) Bank of America. Thanks to all the mergers and stock splits, my accidental 800 shares slowly morphed into 2,100 shares of BofA.

Now? With Bank of America stock trading around $40 a share, that random phone call mistake turned into about $84,000.

So yeah, one misheard word turned into the best "oops" of my financial life.

14

Think Like a Scholar, Borrow Like a Strategist

Let's get one thing straight:

There's no other loan on Earth where an 18-year-old with zero income, zero assets, and zero credit can borrow tens of thousands of dollars . . . no questions asked.

No job? No problem.

No idea how much you'll earn after college? Doesn't matter. Here's $60,000. Sign here.

Oh, you need more for living expenses, books, or off-campus rent? Sure. Sign here and here.

Sound ridiculous? That's the student loan system, and it's real.

The Reality: A Debt Crisis Disguised as Opportunity

Student loan debt in America has ballooned into a $1.77 trillion monster.

That's trillion with a "T." And it's growing every day.

Let's break it down:

- Average Federal & Private Student Loan debt = $41,618
- 42.7 million student borrowers have federal loan debt[1]

---

1. Melanie Hanson, "Student Loan Debt Statistics [2025]," *Education Data Initiative*, March 16, 2025, https://educationdata.org/student-loan-debt-statistics.

- Federal interest rates as of 2025[2]:
  - Undergraduate: 6.53%
  - Graduate: 8.08%
- Tuition hikes in the last two decades[3]:
  - +133% at public colleges
  - +126% at private colleges

Confusing. Chaotic. Crippling.

But here's what really stings: *Almost half of millennials with student loans say college wasn't even worth it.*[4]

Let that sink in.

After years of paused payments during the pandemic, borrowers were told to start repaying. But what followed was chaos[5]:

✗ People got bills twice as high as they expected.

✗ 4+ million borrowers became delinquent.

✗ Another 1+ million are stuck in limbo, waiting for their payment plans to be processed.

✗ The Department of Education was overwhelmed, and customer service lines had 2+ hour hold times.

And get this: Even people who *wanted to pay* couldn't get clear answers or consistent bills.

It's not just a payment problem; it's a broken system. And it probably won't be fixed anytime soon.

What Even *Is* a Student Loan?

Let's break it down.

---

2. "Interest Rates and Fees for Federal Student Loans," FederalStudentAid, https://studentaid.gov/understand-aid/types/loans/interest-rates

3. Sarah Wood, "A look at 20 years of tuition costs at National Universities," *U.S. News*, September 24, 2024, https://www.usnews.com/education/best-colleges/paying-for-college/articles/see-20-years-of-tuition-growth-at-national-universities.

4. Hillary Hoffower, "Nearly Half of Indebted Millennials Say College Wasn't Worth It, and the Reason Why Is Obvious," *Business Insider*, April 11, 2019, https://www.businessinsider.com/personal-finance/millennials-college-not-worth-student-loan-debt-2019-4.

5. Michael Barbaro, "Is the Era of Student Loan Forgiveness Officially Over?" *The Daily*, *The New York Times*, April 21, 2025, https://www.nytimes.com/2025/04/21/podcasts/the-daily/student-loan-forgiveness.html.

A **student loan** is money you borrow to pay for college, and you have to pay it back, with **interest.**

That means:

- If you borrow $20,000 . . .
- You might actually repay $25,000–$30,000+ depending on interest and how fast you pay it off.

Student loans feel like the final boss battle—massive, unavoidable, and way harder if you didn't prepare earlier in the game.

The Real Cost of Borrowing

Here's what a typical student loan might look like:

Loan Amount	Interest Rate	Monthly Payment	Total Paid Over 10 Years
$10,000	6%	$111	$13,322
$25,000	6%	$278	$33,305
$50,000	6%	$556	$66,610

That extra $3k–$16k? That's just *interest*—money you paid to borrow money.

What Makes Student Loans So Dangerous?

Let's keep it real. Student loans aren't like credit cards or car loans. They're worse.

Here's why:

- ✗ You can't return the degree if it doesn't lead to a job.
- ✗ Many students are not fully informed before taking it on.
- ✗ Bankruptcy? Doesn't wipe out student loans like other types of debt.
- ✗ Interest can stack up while you're still in school.
- ✗ Repayment plans are confusing and constantly changing.

× The emotional toll can delay dreams, milestones, and mental health.

In short, student loans can become a lifetime burden, and most people don't understand that until it's too late.

Because this crisis is real. It's not about fear—it's about facts. And knowing this now means you can make smarter choices before you ever sign that dotted line.

Don't let a system designed for confusion rob you of your freedom. You're not powerless, but you *are* responsible for understanding the game before you play it.

Common Student Loan Traps (and How to Dodge Them)

Borrowing More Than You Need
Just because you *qualify* for a $20,000 loan doesn't mean you should take it.

> **Pro Tip:** Only borrow what you actually need for tuition, fees, books, and essentials. Not for vacations or spring break.

Not Knowing Your Career ROI (Return on Investment)
If your future job pays $35,000/year and you graduate with $60,000 in loans . . . that math doesn't work out.

> **Pro Tip:** Research your major's average starting salary *before* borrowing big.

Skipping the Fine Print

Some students don't fully understand the **terms of their loan**— like when payments start, what the interest rate is, or whether it's federal or private. That confusion can cost you big time.

> **Pro Tip:** Know what kind of loan you're signing. Federal loans usually have better repayment options. Private loans? Riskier.

Ignoring Interest While in School

Many student loans start collecting interest right away, even if you don't have to make payments yet. That means your balance is quietly growing while you're in class, eating ramen, and stressing about finals.

> **Pro Tip:** If you can, pay even a small amount of interest while you're in school—it'll save you hundreds (or thousands) later.

Delaying Payments for Too Long

It's tempting to delay payments after graduation using grace periods or deferment. But remember: **interest often keeps growing** in the background.

> **Pro Tip:** If you're able, start making small payments as soon as possible—even during grace periods.

Using Loans for Lifestyle

Some students use leftover loan money for shopping, upgrades, or fancy living. But every dollar you spend now could cost you double later.

> **Pro Tip:** If you wouldn't buy it with cash, don't buy it with loans. Please, for the love, don't just let your student loan money sit in your savings account if you don't need it right away. While it's sitting there, interest is adding up, and you'll have to pay back more than you borrowed.

FAFSA, Grants, and Scholarships = Free Money First

Before you even *think* about borrowing:

1. **Fill out the FAFSA**—It's your gateway to federal aid like grants, loans, and work-study.
2. **Apply for scholarships**—Local, national, weird ones— every bit helps
3. **Look for grants**—These are based on need or merit, and don't need to be paid back.
4. **Start early**—You can start applying for scholarships as early as 9th grade!

Need-to-Know Loan Lingo

Term	What It Means
Subsidized Loan	The government pays interest while you're in school. ✔ Better option.
Unsubsidized Loan	You're charged interest from day 1. It adds up fast.
Interest	The cost of borrowing money—usually a percentage of your loan.
Loan Servicer	The company that manages your loan and accepts your payments.
Deferment	Temporary pause on payments (but sometimes interest still grows).

The 4 Main Types of Financial Aid

Type	What It Means
Grants	Free money (usually from the government) that you don't repay. Based mostly on income.
Scholarships	Also free. Based on grades, talents, interests, background, or just for applying!
Work-Study	A part-time job on campus that helps cover expenses. Flexible and student-friendly.
Loans	Money you borrow now and pay back later with interest. Use wisely.

Some of it's free.

Some of it you work for.

Some you have to pay back (so choose carefully).

Scholarships = Free Money. Go Get It

There are scholarships for having good grades, playing sports, being in a club, being first-gen college student, volunteering, etc.

Where to Find Them:

- School counselor (they know more than you think)
- Local businesses and community organizations
- Online:
  - scholarships.com
  - appily.com
  - fastweb.com
  - raise.me
  - bigfuture.collegeboard.org
  - dosomething.org

How to Apply:

1. Find a scholarship you're eligible for.
2. Write a short essay, fill out a form, or make videos (yes, really).
3. Submit before the deadline.
4. Repeat. And repeat again.

It's estimated that over $100 million in scholarship money goes unused each year.[6] That's free money just sitting there.

Your Before-You-Borrow Checklist

Before signing that loan agreement, ask:

- ☐ Do I understand what this will cost me per month after graduation?
- ☐ Have I looked at my major's potential salary?
- ☐ Have I applied for at least 10 scholarships?
- ☐ Do I know what subsidized vs. unsubsidized means?
- ☐ Am I borrowing only what I need?

---

6. Sarah Brooks, "A Guide to Unclaimed Scholarships and Grants," SoFi, May 27, 2025, https://www.sofi.com/learn/content/unclaimed-scholarship-guide/.

If you answered "no" to any of those—pause, research, and rethink.

College can be a powerful investment, but only if you treat it like one. Don't take out loans blindly. Don't borrow for things you don't need. Think like a scholar. Borrow like a strategist.

LEVEL UP

Student loans can help you move forward or hold you back. The difference? A smart plan. Grab your journal and reflect on the following thoughts.

Why do you want to go to college? Be honest.

Think about what life after college might feel like if you had to pay $400+/month in loan payments. What would that delay or limit?

Check all the steps you've taken (or will commit to):

☐ **Researched the average starting salary for my major**

☐ **Compared total cost of attendance at 3+ schools**

☐ **Applied for FAFSA, grants, and at least 3 scholarships**

☐ **Learned the difference between subsidized and unsubsidized loans**

☐ **Calculated how much I actually need, not just how much I can borrow**

☐ **Talk to a counselor or trusted adult about borrowing smart**

☐ **Create a college budget plan before applying for loans**

CARLEY RAINS

I still remember sitting at college orientation, excited and ready to take the next step, until my parents looked at me and said: *"Carley, we can't afford to pay for your college. You'll have to cover it yourself."*

It hit like a ton of bricks. I had great grades, was third in my class, involved in everything. I applied to over 100 scholarships. And guess what?

I got zero.

Then I opened my financial aid package from Texas Tech. No scholarships. Just student loans.

It was crushing. I was embarrassed. I had my dorm picked, roommate set, and decorations bought. But the thought of taking on all that debt made my stomach drop. So I made a decision that honestly scared me:

I unenrolled. No backup. No clear plan. Just a strong feeling that debt wasn't the right path for me.

With little over a month left of school, I searched and searched for college options and gap programs that were affordable. The issue was I only had a couple hundred dollars to my name.

Weeks later, my mom got a random call at 10:30 p.m. from a college coach who said, "I see that Carley was involved in track. I think with proper training she could be a great distance runner."

I couldn't believe it. *Me? Run in college?* All I could think was how many miles I'd have to run.

I was hesitant, but eventually I said yes, more out of curiosity than confidence.

The offer? A $1 scholarship.

That's right. *One single dollar.*

But there was potential to earn more. Walk-ons only earn funding if they outperform scholarship athletes. Since I already had a scholarship, I just had to maintain or improve my performance to keep it. It opened a door. I joined the team. I trained hard. And slowly, that opportunity grew. By the time I graduated, that $1 scholarship turned into full funding.

It wasn't the plan I started with. It wasn't what I expected. But it turned out to be exactly what I needed.

Sometimes, chasing your goals means making scary decisions, taking a weird side road, or saying yes to something you're not totally sure about. You don't have to have it all figured out. Just be willing to bet on yourself and keep moving forward.

A WORD FROM
SOFIA BUITRAGO

When I first chose to go to college in Florida, it was mostly about the price. I had in-state tuition, and financially, that made the most sense. I started my degree online in 2020 from Germany, right as COVID hit. After a year, I moved to the US to continue in person at the University of West Florida, but pretty quickly, I realized it didn't feel right. Even though I'm American, I was born in Germany and grew up around European culture. I missed it more than I expected.

After two years in Florida, I moved back to Germany, finished classes online, and started thinking seriously about transferring to a university in Europe. I spent time researching schools, watching YouTube videos, reading student reviews, and eventually visiting a few places in person. That's how I found the American University of Paris (AUP), where I'm now finishing my degree. (There are plenty of other American university campuses too in Rome, Cairo, Bulgaria, etc.)

The transition wasn't instant or easy, but it was absolutely worth it. AUP is an American-style university, so all my classes are in English, but I also get to take French and be surrounded by people from all over the world. That international environment was exactly what I was craving. I've met students from countries I'd never even been to, and I've learned just as much outside the classroom as I have in it.

Living in Paris has its own challenges, of course. Exchange rates are an important factor to consider. It's not cheap, but it's different from the expenses I had in Florida. I don't need a car here, so I save money on gas, insurance, and repairs. Public transportation is cheap for students, and the city is walkable and bike-friendly. I've learned how to find affordable housing, save money by grocery shopping at local markets, and make the most of student discounts for everything from museums to food. Tuition at AUP is higher than in-state tuition in Florida, but the school accepts FAFSA and American financial aid, which helped make it possible.

If you're thinking about studying abroad, here's what I'll say: Be honest with yourself about what kind of experience you want. Don't just go where everyone else is going. Think about the kind of lifestyle that makes you feel most like *you*. Don't be afraid to change paths, and don't stress if you don't have it all figured out yet. I didn't, and I still ended up in the right place. What matters most is being open to change, doing your homework, and making choices based on who you are and how you want to grow. For me, that meant leaving the US and finishing my degree in Paris, and I'm so glad I did.

A WORD FROM
LEVI ELLISON

When my wife and I graduated from pharmacy school in May 2018, we were pumped.

Together, we landed jobs making $265,000 a year. That's a quarter million dollars!

We felt like we had *made it*.

But here's what didn't feel so good: We also walked out with $208,000 in student loan debt. And the interest alone was adding over $1,000 a month. Just for . . . existing.

So yeah, we were making great money. But a lot of it was already spoken for, and we wanted freedom from that. We wanted to live differently, give generously, and not be chained to monthly payments for the next 20 years.

We went after our debt like our hair was on fire.

Over 17 months, we paid off $214,594.55, which is more than $400 a day.

And how did we pull that off?

Two words: budgeting hard.

- We made a written budget *before* every month started.
- We attacked our loans from smallest to largest (a strategy called the debt snowball).
- We barely ate out—maybe 5 times total, on our own dime, the entire 17 months.
- We still gave gifts for birthdays and holidays, but they were part of the plan.
- We gave to causes we believed in, and all within the budget.

People thought we weren't living.

The truth? We were just living *on purpose.*

Now that we're debt free, we get to decide where our money goes. It doesn't disappear into student loan black holes or rack up interest anymore.

We *own* our income.

And here's the thing: It's totally worth it. The short-term sacrifice gave us long-term freedom.

If you ever get tired of being broke or stressed about money, just know: You *can* pay the price to win.

15

Retire in Style

What if your *future self* could thank you now? Imagine checking your bank account at age 50 and seeing a million bucks sitting there. All because you started early . . . like *high school* early.

You don't need to be a genius or make six figures. You just need time, consistency, and a secret weapon called **compound interest**. Let's go.

What Even *Is* Retirement?

Retirement doesn't mean being old and bored. It means you can stop working when *you* want to and still afford to live your best life.

There's even a whole movement called FIRE, which stands for Financial Independence, Retire Early. It's a growing community (with blogs, YouTube channels, and entire Reddit threads) made up of people who are trying to save and invest so aggressively that they can retire decades before the usual age.[1]

Now, I'm not saying you need to go full-on extreme like some FIRE followers. You don't have to track every penny or live off instant noodles. But being intentional and starting now, instead of waiting, can buy you something way more valuable than stuff: freedom.

---

1. Elizabeth Ayoola, "Fire Movement: What It Is, How It Works," NerdWallet, April 11, 2025, https://www.nerd wallet.com/article/investing/financial-independence-retire-early.

Building good money habits early can unlock big dreams later, like:

- Traveling the world (without checking your bank app every five minutes)
- Launching that business you've always dreamed of
- Volunteering full time for a cause you care about
- Chilling on a beach . . . with your laptop closed and no Zoom calls in sight
- Taking care of your parents or loved ones without financial stress
- Buying your dream home or a cozy cabin in the woods
- Sending your kids to college without student loans (or helping a niece/nephew do the same)
- Funding a passion project—music, writing, art—without waiting for a paycheck
- Building generational wealth, so your future family gets a head start

The Rule of 72

Can I get a hoorah for compound interest!?

Why are we bringing this term up *again?* Because if money had a secret weapon, *this is it.* And this is what will propel you toward retirement.

Enter: The Rule of 72.

The Rule of 72 is a quick, back-pocket math trick to figure out how long it'll take for your money to double with compound interest.

Here's the formula:

72 ÷ your interest rate = years to double your money

So let's say you invest money and earn a 10% interest rate each year.

$$72 \div 10 = 7.2 \text{ years}$$

That means your money will double in just over 7 years. Example:

- You invest $1,000 at 10% interest.
- In about 7 years, it becomes $2,000.
- In another 7 years, it becomes $4,000.
- Another 7, is now $8,000.

That's compound interest doing its thing—your money earns interest, then *that* interest earns interest.

Now, just for kicks and giggles . . .

Let's say you have $200,000 invested with 10% interest. In just about 7 years, that $200,000 becomes $400,000 without adding a single extra dollar.

Give it another 7 years? Boom. $800,000.

Another 7? You're knocking on the door of $1.6 million.

This is why starting young is a major power move. The earlier you start, the more doubling time you give your money. The more money you add, the more it has to work with. Magic.

Enter the Roth IRA: Your Teen Superpower

A Roth IRA is a retirement account. But it's not just for old people; it's perfect for teens with jobs.

Why?

- You pay taxes *now* (when your income is low)
- Your money grows tax free
- You can pull out your contributions *anytime*
- Withdrawals in retirement? Also *tax free*

Meet Suzi the Babysitter

- Suzi starts saving $2,000/year in a Roth IRA at age 14.
- She stops saving after 6 years at age 20.
- Let's say she never touches it again.

If her investments grow at an average of 10% per year (which is close to the historical average of the stock market[2]), then by the time she turns 60, her Roth IRA could be worth nearly $1 million.

And she only invested $12,000 total.

That's the power of starting early. Time did most of the work for her.

Heck yeah.

Your Quick Start Plan

1. Get a job (babysitting, side hustle, mowing lawns, etc.).
2. Open a **Roth IRA** (if you are a minor, ask a guardian for help). You will need your Social Security number.
3. Put in part of your earnings (even $20/month is great). Invest in a **simple index fund** in the Roth (like a total market ETF).
4. Chill. Let time and compound growth do their thing.

Tools to Help You Start Investing[3]

Here are beginner-friendly platforms where you can open a Roth IRA or start investing, even with small amounts. Each offers low-cost or no-cost options and is designed to help new investors learn as they grow.

---

2. James Royal, "The Average Stock Market Return," NerdWallet, April 10, 2025, https://www.nerdwallet.com /article/investing/average-stock-market-return.
3. Alana Benson, "Best Roth IRAs Right Now: Top Picks for 2025," NerdWallet, May 1, 2025, https://www.nerd wallet.com/best/investing/roth-ira-accounts.

#1 pick: Robinhood

- Super user-friendly app
- Easy, step-by-step setup for opening a Roth IRA
- No account minimums or commissions
- Lets you invest in stocks, ETFs, and more with just a few taps
- You can also invest in index funds outside of a Roth in just a few clicks
- Allows for all of your investments in one place

> **Be cautious:** It can feel like a game and lead to impulsive decisions.

Fidelity

- No account minimums or trading fees
- Offers Youth Accounts (ages 13–17) with Roth IRA access once you have earned income
- Includes strong educational tools and support

Charles Schwab

- No minimum balance required and no fees for Roth IRAs
- User-friendly mobile app and strong learning platform
- Accounts for minors must be opened with a parent or guardian

Vanguard

- Known for low-cost index funds and long-term investing
- Ideal for a "set-it-and-forget-it" approach
- Interface is more basic, but the platform is reliable and respected

Betterment

- Automated investing based on your goals and risk level
- Great for hands-off investors who want simplicity
- Charges a 0.25% annual management fee

But what if I need the money?

No worries. You can always pull out your contributions (not the earnings) without fees or taxes. It can even help with:

- College
- Emergencies
- A down payment on your first home

Still, the goal? Let it ride. The longer your money grows, the bigger the payoff.

Challenge: Out-Save Your Parents

Ask them how much they've saved for retirement. Then tell them about your Roth IRA plan.

They'll be impressed. Or shook. Or both.

Recap: Why Roth IRAs Rock for Teens and Young Adults

- Tax-free growth for decades
- Contributions are always accessible
- You don't need much to start
- You're literally building a millionaire future

Start early, and money works for you.
Start late, and you work for money.
Boom. Now you know the secret. Time to use it.

LEVEL UP

Want future-you to live free instead of working forever? I get it . . . retirement feels like it's light-years away. But trust me, it sneaks up faster than you'd ever expect. Reflect on the following in your journal.

What's one thing you'd love to be able to do without worrying about money when you're older?

ROTH IRA REALITY CHECK

Do you have any kind of income right now?

- ☐ **Yes—I'm ready to start a Roth IRA**
- ☐ **No—but I'll plan for when I do**

Choose one step you'll take this week:

- ☐ **Talk to a parent about opening a custodial Roth IRA**
- ☐ **Research a Roth account platform (Robinhood, Fidelity, Vanguard, etc.)**
- ☐ **Set a savings goal (even $20/month!) to invest once I can**
- ☐ **Use the Rule of 72 to see how fast my money could double**
- ☐ **Watch a beginner video about how Roth IRAs work**

This week, I will: _____

A WORD FROM
MARY CONLAN

I always thought working hard and doing the right thing would protect me. But at 62, after decades of steady work, I was suddenly laid off. The company brought in younger people, and just like that, I was out.

Competing for jobs in your 60s against people in their 40s? It's tough. It took me six months and nearly 200 job applications to find something new.

The only reason I stayed afloat? I had savings and passive income from an Airbnb I started at age 57. That earned me enough money a month to help cover my bills while I job hunted.

My advice? Start early.

Learn about passive income. Build up savings. Use your travel rewards. Read books that grow your mindset. Don't wait until life forces you to figure it out.

Also? Working out, eating right, and taking care of yourself matters more than you think. Age is a number, but people still judge by appearances. Stay sharp, stay ready.

Retirement shouldn't catch you off guard. And trust me, you don't want to find yourself both too young to retire and too old to get hired.

A WORD FROM
SHANE KINSLOW

After college, I had a buddy who said he could hook me up with a job in the area. It would've been easy, comfortable, and familiar. But something in me just couldn't settle for that. I wanted to see the world, not stay planted in the same place I grew up.

The Air Force had always been in the back of my mind. So one day, I did what any curious 20-something does, I Googled: "Best Air Force jobs for traveling."

That's how I found out about being a boom operator. The job? Refueling aircraft mid-air. Literally flying at high altitudes and connecting fuel lines between planes in flight. You travel constantly. Wherever the jets go, you go—around the country and across the globe. I thought, "This is it."

I walked into the recruiter's office and told him straight up, "I want to be a boom operator."

They told me I had to list a few options, but I got lucky and that job became my job.

Since then, I've been stationed in Arkansas, California, Japan, and Germany. I've watched the sunrise from the back of a KC-10 in a different country more times than I can count.

And while all of that is amazing, here's what really blew my mind once I got in:

The money game.

A lot of people don't realize that the military sets you up for long-term financial success, if you're smart about it. I started investing in the Thrift Savings Plan (TSP) right away. It's like a 401(k) but with **matching contributions** up to 5% and major tax benefits.

Plus, I get free healthcare, housing allowances, and some serious travel perks.

But here's the part that still feels surreal: If I stay in for 20 years, I retire at 45 with 40% of my base pay *for life.*

Every. Single. Month.

Not to mention, I still have my GI Bill. I could go back for a master's degree if I wanted. For free.

I didn't plan this out from day one. I just knew I wanted something different. And now, I'm on track to retire before most people even hit their career stride.

16

Reinvention:
Your Secret Weapon

The world is changing—Fast.

We're living in one of the most transformational times in history. Technology, especially artificial intelligence and automation, is reshaping the way we learn, work, and earn.

This isn't about the future. It's happening right now.

Consider the following from the World Economic Forum[1]:

- By the end of the decade, 9 million jobs are expected to be displaced by AI.
- At the same time, about 11 million new jobs will be created; many which have never existed.
- Smart technology is becoming a normal part of how work gets done and will likely reshape every career sector.

Roles like cashiers, bank tellers, data entry clerks, drivers (thanks to autonomous vehicles), assembly line workers, customer service agents, and basic clerical jobs are shrinking fast—replaced by automation, AI, and robots.

Why? Because they're repetitive, follow clear rules, and can easily be done by technology.

---

1. "The Future of Jobs Report 2025," World Economic Forum, May 2023, https://www.weforum.org/publications/the-future-of-jobs-report-2025/.

Imagine you're a writer, artist, or someone who helps companies come up with creative ways to promote their products. Now imagine AI stepping in and doing some of that work faster, cheaper, and 24/7. Sounds a little intimidating, right?

But here's the good news: while AI is replacing some roles, it's *also* creating brand-new ones. The people who will win in this new world? Those who learn how to *work with* AI instead of ignoring it or fearing it.

You don't need to be a tech wizard or build robots in your garage. You just need to start getting familiar with the tools shaping the future.

But jobs that rely on *creativity, critical thinking, empathy,* and *problem-solving*? Those are a lot harder to automate, and that's where the opportunity is.

> "Anything that can be automated will be automated. Anything that requires judgment, empathy, or innovation will become more valuable."
>
> —*Thomas L. Friedman*

In short: Robots can count inventory. But they can't build trust, dream up a new idea, or lead a team—not yet, anyway.

That's why building the *right* skills matters more than ever.

Future-Proof Skills That Will Make You Unstoppable[2]

If you want a career that's flexible, profitable, and exciting, then invest in skills that AI can't easily copy, such as:

→ **Creativity:** Thinking outside the box and imagining what doesn't exist yet

---

2. David O'Hara, "Why People Skills Are Still Important in the Age of AI," Forbes, May 2, 2024, https://www.forbes.com/councils/forbesbusinesscouncil/2024/05/02/why-people-skills-are-still-important-in-the-age-of-ai/.

→ **Critical Thinking:** Solving complex, real-world problems
→ **Leadership:** Inspiring and guiding others toward a goal
→ **Communication:** Speaking and writing clearly and persuasively
→ **Emotional Intelligence:** Understanding people and building strong relationships
→ **Digital Fluency:** Using tech tools comfortably and confidently

These are called *transferable skills*, which means they go with you no matter what job, career, or industry you end up in.

Where to Learn and Hone Skills

Free or Affordable Courses

Coursera	College-level courses from top universities (many are free)
Udemy	Affordable, skill-based courses in tech, business, and more
edX	Ivy League classes, including Harvard and MIT
Khan Academy	Free learning in math, science, finance, and more
LinkedIn Learning	Great for professional skills and certifications
Skillshare	Creative courses (animation, writing, video editing, etc.)
Google Digital Garage	Free training in digital skills and marketing
FutureLearn	Global learning platform with career-focused courses
Codecademy	Learn to code, even as a complete beginner
MIT OpenCourseWare	Free college-level courses from MIT

AI Tools for Writing, Research, and Brainstorming

ChatGPT	Help with essays, brainstorming, and understanding tough topics
Claude	Great for summarizing long texts and keeping context
Perplexity AI	Fast, cited answers for research questions
Microsoft Copilot	Smart writing and spreadsheet help in Word/Excel
Jasper	Great for content creating
Scite	Pulls academic research and builds proper citations
Elicit	AI research assistant, ideal for scientific writing and planning

AI for Visuals, Video, and Design

Midjourney	Creates high-quality AI art and illustrations
DALL·E	Turns text into creative images
Runway ML	Tools for AI video editing and motion design
Pika Labs	Create short AI-generated videos from prompts
Canva Magic Studio	Easy designs and presentations with AI features
Adobe Firefly	AI-powered image editing and effects
Krea.ai	Real-time AI art and enhancing videos and images

AI Tools for Learning, Planning, and Coding

GitHub Copilot	Helps you write and understand code
Notion AI	Plans projects, generates content, and organizes thoughts
Google Gemini (formerly Bard)	Creative writing and coding assistant
Replit Ghostwriter	Code assistant inside a live coding environment
Khanmigo	AI tutor from Khan Academy (great for STEM and coding help)

AI for Audio, Content, and Media

Descript	Recording, transcribing, editing, and sharing videos and podcasts
Copy.ai	Fast content creation for blogs, emails, and social media
ElevenLabs	Makes content universally accessible in any language and in any voice
CapCut (with AI)	Quick mobile video editing, great for social media
Otter.ai	Real-time transcription for lectures, meetings, or interviews

Keep an eye out because new online tools and programs are launching all the time. They're not just fun to explore; they're powerful learning tools. The sooner you get comfortable using them, the more of an edge you'll have in school, work, and beyond.

Back in the 1990s, not many people knew how to use Microsoft Excel. But the ones who did? They became super valuable.

The same thing is happening today with AI tools. If you learn how to use them now, you'll stand out later.

You don't have to be a programmer tomorrow. But you *do* need to start learning the tools that will keep you in the game. Ignoring AI now is like refusing to learn how to drive when everyone else already has a car.

Reinvention = Your Career Survival Skill

What's reinvention?

It's the ability to shift gears, learn something new, or change direction when life, or the job market, demands it.

You won't just need one career. You'll likely have many, and that's okay.

People who thrive in this new world are the ones who can:

- Take on different roles
- Stay relevant as the world evolves
- Find multiple ways to make money
- Always learn new skills
- Know when to pivot instead of panic

Reinvention isn't just a *nice-to-have*—it's your secret weapon.

It doesn't mean starting over.

A lot of people think "reinventing yourself" means throwing everything away and starting from scratch.

Not true.

It's not about wiping your life clean; it's about leveling up.

In a world that's constantly changing, your education doesn't end with a diploma.

To stay ready for anything, you'll need to keep learning, and not with pop quizzes and lockers, but in real-life, hands-on, curiosity-driven ways.

And one more thing, don't fall for get-rich-quick schemes. If it promises big money with little effort, it's probably a scam. Real success comes from building skills, solving real problems, and staying consistent. Lifelong learners don't chase shortcuts. Instead, they build strong foundations that last.

Lifelong Learning in Action

Podcasts

The Inforium (formerly The College Info Geek Podcast)	A show about productivity, personal finance, entrepreneurship, and various other interesting things
TED Talks Daily	Brings the latest TED Talks on a variety of topics, perfect for staying inspired and informed
The Mindset Mentor	Centers on developing motivation, direction, and focus in life
How I Built This With Guy Raz	Interviews with entrepreneurs and innovators, sharing their journey of building successful ventures
Financial Feminist	A show about making more, spending less, and feeling financially confident; target audience is women

Social Media Influencers

Instagram	@personalfinanceclub @pricelesstay @herfirst100k @the.brokegeneration @mrmoneymustache
TikTok	@humphreytalks @marktilbury @yourrichbff @thebudgetnista

YouTube Channels

Ali Abdaal	Shares insights on effective learning, time management, and career growth
Graham Stephan	Former real estate agent turned finance YouTuber; breaks down credit cards, investing, and how to build wealth early
Nate O'Brien	Minimalist and money-savvy, teaches budgeting, simple living, and long-term investing for beginners
Humphrey Yang	Known for breaking down complex financial topics (like taxes, stock market basics, and inflation) in an easy-to-understand way
Her First $100k (Tori Dunlap)	Financial education focused on women and Gen Z; covers saving, investing, and fighting financial inequality
Minority Mindset (Jaspreet Singh)	Talks entrepreneurship, saving, investing, and the mindset shift needed to escape living paycheck to paycheck
Rich & Regular	A couple sharing their journey to financial independence and FIRE (Financial Independence, Retire Early)

Warning: Social media can be a fun way to learn, but when it comes to money, *be extra careful.*

"FinanceTok" and other online platforms are filled with advice, but a lot of it is based on myths, half-truths, or even straight-up scams. Some creators look trustworthy but are just trying to go viral or sell you something.

Just because someone talks confidently doesn't mean they know what they're doing. Always double-check financial advice with trusted sources: a teacher, a certified financial expert, or reliable websites. Learning about money is powerful, but learning it the *right way* is what really sets you apart.

LEVEL UP

In a world that's constantly moving, your ability to adapt is your greatest superpower.

But just as important? The ability to think for yourself.

Be wise. Be alert. Not everything you hear, especially online, is true.

Misinformation is everywhere, especially when it comes to money and success.

Ask questions. Check sources. Trust your gut, and don't be afraid to dig deeper.

You don't need to have all the answers right now; no one does. What matters is that you stay curious, stay open, and stay ready to grow.

Life will throw you curveballs. Plans will change. Doors will close. But new ones will open, if you're willing to keep showing up and figuring it out.

Keep learning. Keep leveling up.

Reinvention isn't a backup plan. It's the game-changer.

Stay sharp. Stay ready. Start now.

Your future is built one smart move at a time.

Glossary

Appreciable. Something that typically increases in value over time (like a house or some investments).

Assets. Anything you own that has value like money, a car, or investments.

Bonds. A way to lend money to a company or the government and they pay you back with interest.

Cash Equivalents. Very safe, short-term investments that can quickly be turned into cash, like money market accounts.

Certificate of Deposit (CD). A savings account where you agree to keep your money in the bank for a set amount of time (like 6 months or 1 year) in exchange for a higher interest rate. You usually can't take the money out early without paying a penalty. It's a low-risk way to grow your savings slowly.

Compound Interest. Interest that builds on top of interest—like stacking gains every year.

Contributions. The money you put into something like a savings account, Roth IRA, or investment plan.

Cover Letter. A short letter you write when applying for a job that explains why you're a great fit.

Credit. Borrowing money now and agreeing to pay it back later, often with interest.

Credit Card. A card that lets you borrow money to make purchases, which you pay back monthly.

Credit Score. A number (usually 300–850) that shows how trustworthy you are at borrowing and paying back money.

Debit Card. A card that takes money directly from your bank account when you spend it. No borrowing.

Debt. Money you owe to someone else, like from loans or credit cards.

Depreciable. Something that loses value over time, like a car or a phone.

Direct Deposit. A way to get paid where your money goes straight into your bank account—no paper checks, no waiting. Most jobs and government payments use direct deposit so you get your money faster and safely.

Diversification. Spreading your money across different types of investments so you lower your risk.

Dividends. Money that some companies pay you just for owning their stock, like a reward.

Emergency Fund. Money saved for unexpected situations, like car repairs or losing a job.

ETF (Exchange-Traded Fund). A type of investment that's like a bundle of stocks or bonds you can buy and sell like a single stock.

FAFSA (Free Application for Federal Student Aid). The form students fill out to apply for college financial aid, including grants and loans.

Financing. When you borrow money to pay for something now and agree to pay it back later, usually with interest. Financing is commonly used for big purchases like cars, college, or furniture. It can seem helpful in the moment, but it often means you end up paying more over time than the item originally cost.

401(k). A retirement savings plan some employers offer. You can have money taken out of your paycheck (before taxes) and invested for the future. This lowers taxable income now, but you will have to pay taxes in the future when you take it out. Maximum you can contribute. $23,000 a year. Some employers match what you put in. Free money for retirement!

High-Yield Savings Account. A type of savings account that pays a much higher interest rate than a traditional savings account, helping your money grow faster over time.

Inflation. When prices go up over time, making your money buy less than before.

Index Fund. An investment that automatically follows a group of companies, like the top 500 in the stock market.

Interest. Extra money paid for borrowing money or earned when you save or invest.

Interview. A conversation where an employer asks you questions to see if you're right for the job.

Liabilities. Money you owe like loans, bills, or credit card balances.

Lifestyle Creep. When you start spending more money as you earn more, instead of saving it.

Liquid Net Assets. The money and investments you can quickly turn into cash, minus what you owe.

Matching Contributions. Money that your employer adds to your retirement account (like a 401(k)) to match some of the money you put in, usually up to a certain percentage. It's basically free money your job gives you for saving for the future. Major job perk.

Mutual Funds. An investment where people pool their money together to buy a mix of stocks and bonds.

Negative Compound Interest. When debt builds on itself because interest keeps adding up and you don't pay it off.

Net Worth. What you own (assets) minus what you owe (liabilities). It's your financial scorecard.

Networking. Building relationships with people who can help you with advice, jobs, or opportunities.

Opportunity Cost. What you give up when you choose one option over another, like spending now vs. saving for later.

Price of a Share. The current cost to buy one share of a company's stock. This price goes up and down based on how the company is doing and how much people want to buy or sell it.

Resume. A one-page summary of your skills, education, and experience that you give to employers.

Return on Investment (ROI). A way to measure if something was worth the money or time you spent on it—did it pay off?

Roth IRA. A retirement savings account where your money grows and you can withdraw it (and earnings) when you retire, completely tax-free. Maximum you can contribute. $7,000 a year.

S&P 500. A list of 500 big U.S. companies used to measure how the stock market is doing.

Savings Account. A bank account that helps you save money and earn a little interest over time.

Share. A single unit of ownership in a company. When you buy a share, you own a small piece of that company.

Stock Market. Where people buy and sell shares of companies. A place to invest and grow money.

Stocks. Pieces of a company that you can buy. If the company does well, your stock can grow in value.

Student Loans. Money you borrow to pay for school and you have to pay it back later with interest.

Time Value of Money. The idea that money now is worth more than the same amount later because it can grow over time.

Tuition. The cost you pay to take classes at a college or university. It usually covers instruction, professors, and access to academic resources but not housing, meals, books, or other fees.

Acknowledgments

Thank you to all the contributors who generously shared their personal stories about money. Your honesty, insight, and experiences have added depth and heart to this book. We're grateful for your voices and the impact they'll have on future readers.

About the Authors

Lindsey Baker, MAT

Lindsey Baker is a licensed teacher and writer with a passion for helping the next generation build strong foundations in life and money. With over a decade of experience in education, she has taught students in Arkansas, California, the West Bank, Turkey, and Germany. Lindsey focuses on making complex topics accessible, engaging, and empowering for young learners.

email: themoneycheatcode@gmail.com
TikTok: @themoneycheatcode
Instagram: @themoneycheatcode
Website: themoneycheatcode.com

Joe Baker, MBA

Joe Baker is a longtime educator and advocate for financial literacy. With over twenty years of experience teaching personal finance at the university level and nearly three decades in the insurance and financial services industry, Joe brings a wealth of real-world insight to his work. He has spoken to audiences across the country, helping individuals and professionals make smarter financial choices.

I would appreciate your feedback on what chapters helped you most and what you would like to see in future books.

If you enjoyed this book and found it helpful, please leave a review on Amazon.

Visit me at

THEMONEYCHEATCODE.COM

where you can sign up for email updates.

THANK YOU!

www.ingramcontent.com/pod-product-compliance
Lightning Source LLC
Chambersburg PA
CBHW071642210326
41597CB00017B/2088